HOW TO
LIVE WITH A MAN*

and love it!

JENNIFER WORICK

The only thing author Jennifer Worick loves more than men is writing about them. She is the co-author of the *New York Times* bestseller *The Worst-Case Scenario Survival Handbook: Dating & Sex* and *The Action Heroine's Handbook,* among many other publications. She lives in Philadelphia.

HOW TO
LIVE WITH A MAN*

JENNIFER WORICK

*and love it!

KEY PORTER BOOKS

This edition published by Key Porter Books by arrangement with Elwin Street Limited

2006 Key Porter Books

Copyright © 2005 by Elwin Street Limited

Conceived and produced by
Elwin Street Limited
79 St John Street
London EC1M 4NR
www.elwinstreet.com

Library and Archives Canada Cataloguing in Publication

Worick, Jennifer
    How to live with a man... and love it! /
Jennifer Worick

Includes index.
ISBN 1-55263-770-0

    1. Man-woman relationships. I. Title

HQ801.W67 2006   646.7'8

C2005-903902-7

ONTARIO ARTS COUNCIL
CONSEIL DES ARTS DE L'ONTARIO

THE CANADA COUNCIL   LE CONSEIL DES ARTS
FOR THE ARTS   DU CANADA
SINCE 1957   DEPUIS 1957

The publisher gratefully acknowledges the support of the Canada Council for the Arts and the Ontario Arts Council for its publishing program. We acknowledge the support of the Government of Ontario through the Ontario Media Development Corporation's Ontario Book Initiative.

We acknowledge the financial support of the Government of Canada through the Book Publishing Industry Development Program (BPIDP) for our publishing activities.

Key Porter Books Limited
Six Adelaide Street East, Tenth Floor
Toronto, Ontario
Canada M5C 1H6

Designed by Headcase Design
Edited by Diana Steedman

Printed and bound in Singapore

05 06 07 08 09 5 4 3 2 1

CONTENTS

INTRODUCTION

Nowadays, there is much talk about the "career woman" who has little time for love, or the woman who lives alone and likes it. But deep in the heart of many women lies the urge to love and be loved; to be found desirable in the eyes of a special someone. This is a basic instinct that is hard to shake. And, ladies, why should we shake it? There is nothing to be ashamed of in admitting this instinct, and much happiness is in store for the woman who chooses not to fight her natural inclinations.

How to Live with a Man and Love It! is a godsend to any woman entering into a committed and loving relationship. Packed with the sort of gentle advice that ought to be given out with every engagement ring, it will help you steer a steady course through the rocky straits of married life. Throughout history, ladies have known that planning and strategy can lead to success in matters of the heart. Romance and glamour can survive if common sense is applied at the right time, but the fact is that love alone is not going to produce a happy home. It's necessary, of course, but so too is patience, and good old-fashioned craftiness.

You'll learn how to cope with big issues such as merging households and finances, and with everyday annoyances such as forgotten chores and an obsession with a certain sports team. You'll learn to pick your battles and create new traditions. No topic is off-limits.

But there's still that nagging question in the back of your mind. Are you turning your back on the sisterhood by even picking up this book? Not at all! You know that you are an equal in your relationship. Let's be honest, you are probably superior in many ways. This book will tell you how to get the upper hand and keep it, all the while making your man content and happy.

So read and digest the wisdom in this book; then, with your head held high, and your heart filled with peace, love, and understanding, join the ranks of happy cohabiting couples.

CREATING
A HOME

In this chapter, you'll learn how to:

❋ Decide between his place, your place, and a new place
❋ Choose a location which suits you both ❋ Create romantic rituals
to stay connected ❋ Set up your space for mutual satisfaction
❋ Maintain your independence in your shared space

CREATING A HOME IS MORE THAN DECIDING TO MOVE IN together. It's even more than finding a place, signing a lease, packing the boxes, and hiring the movers. As significant as all that sounds—and it is—in reality, it's the easy part. No matter how much time you might have spent together, once you decide to live with a man, everything changes. There is an escalated sense of commitment, which can be thrilling, but there is also a sharp decline in independence, which may cause "cold feet" and worry.

Creating a home together means accepting both the joy and frustration of sharing your environment. You are cohabiting, and there's no way around it—it's wildly different from dating. It doesn't hurt to have some guidelines to help you make the transition. With some thoughtfulness, planning, and compromise, your house will feel like a home—a home just perfect for two.

Before bringing your two worlds together, first get in touch with your individual selves. You can't begin to navigate different tastes and temperaments until you, as they say, know thyself. So start making lists of your preferences and dislikes. Ask your guy to do the same. List what's important to you in a living space (serious water pressure in the shower, hardwood floors, cleanliness, charm, safety, backyard). Jot down what kind of neighborhood you like (lots of kids, tree-lined sidewalks, a deli or bar on every corner, inquisitive neighbors, and the like). Okay so far? Now, write down what you consider to be your most valuable possessions (your flat-screen television, photo albums, an heirloom necklace). Getting even more personal, make a list of what qualities you value in a roommate, taking the emphasis off your romantic relationship. Now compare lists and discuss. Do you share the same vision for living together? Are you surprised by anything you or he wrote down?

YOUR PLACE OR MINE?

Many couples who decide to share their lives are faced with this dilemma: Do you move into his place, does he move into yours, or do you find somewhere new? There's no easy way to come to a decision on this, especially if you each love your home and are reluctant to let it go. Perhaps you've invested a lot of time and money improving your house; perhaps the market isn't ideal for getting a return on your investment. On the other hand, perhaps his house is more convenient for the office or in a more appealing neighborhood. If there are no obvious tie-breakers (roommate issues, size constraints, financial considerations) for choosing one place over another, you should do the old-fashioned "pros and cons" list for each option.

Try to be objective when discussing these, as well as other issues that are important to you. Is he ever vexed by your noisy neighbors when he comes over? Do you hate walking three flights up to his apartment, especially carrying bags of groceries? Does he love barbecuing on his deck, which isn't possible at your place? Do you relish time in your vegetable garden, which he doesn't have? It all comes down to quality of life, and where you will feel the most comfortable embarking on a new journey together. Be prepared to give up some of your individual desires for the good of the couple. This will not be the last time you will be called upon to do so.

If you are committed to choosing one of your existing homes, keep in mind the psychological ramifications of one person moving in to the other person's space. For example, if your man moves in with you, realize that a woman tends to make her house more of a home than a man does. You might have everything organized and decorated just the way you like it, but you'll have to adjust so that your man doesn't feel as if he's just squeezing his belongings into your existing environment.

Whose place offers the better . . .

✓ Neighborhood?

✓ Floor plan/space for living as a couple?

✓ Value for money?

✓ Potential for future additions to your family, such as a pet or a child?

✓ "Incidentals" such as light, outdoor space, garage, appliances?

The crucial thing is that he should not feel like a guest, but like an equal partner in your home.

Before he moves in, clear plenty of space in drawers and closets, the medicine cabinet, the garage, and even the kitchen cupboards. Take time to walk through each room together, talking about what he likes and doesn't like about the layout, furnishings, and decor, and discussing what could be changed to make him feel more at home. Let him know his comfort is important to you—this shows you are committed to making the move work. If it means ditching the stuffed animals or relegating your antique sewing machine to the closet to make room for his treadmill, do it. (You can always move it back later—he probably won't use the treadmill anyway!)

Joint purchases can also help make the house feel like it belongs to you both. Shop together for the things you decide to add to the home, now that you're in it together—new curtains, a great rug, bedding that pleases both of you, a piece of art to replace your girly floral painting in the bedroom. Upgrading the bathroom tiles or repainting the kitchen can have the same effect. Deciding how much to spend and where to put new purchases will make you feel like a team and give you a sense of accomplishment as a couple—and seeing them every day will remind you of your commitment to live together under one roof.

If instead you move into his place, he will hopefully offer you the same consideration and have space allotted for your wardrobe, personal photos, and beauty products. If not, ease him in slowly and bring up issues gracefully. Be conscious that he may not be used to scented candles, feminine products in the bathroom, and jars of moisturizer on the bedside table. Be respectful of the parts of the home that are his favorites and reflect his taste. No matter how superior you know your taste to be, do not attempt to make over his bachelor pad too quickly—he may balk.

A NEW NEST

The clear benefit of choosing a new place, rather than moving into your place or his, is the feeling that it really belongs to you as a couple. Hunting for your new love nest will reveal much about each other. What is most important to each of you when looking for a home? You may be surprised by each other's answers. Think about the following list, and then rate each criterion from 1 to 10 in order of importance. Once you are aware of your priorities, you will be better armed to find the right place for both you and your man. Simply look for a place that meets each of your top-priority needs.

Priorities	His Rating	Her Rating
Cost	1	3
Location/neighborhood	3	2
Charm/attractiveness	2	1
Size/number of rooms		
Yard/outdoor space		
Amount of sunlight		
Pet-friendly		
Closet space		
Room to grow (space for children)		
Garage		
Distance to work		

After assessing the basic priorities, try to fantasize together about your ideal home. What do you agree on, and what surprises you about your man's vision? What does his fantasy tell you about him? And can you picture yourself living there? Even if you're not able to move into a dream house right away, it's fun to picture it—and it can tell you a great deal about what you both envision for your shared future. Does your man want a Hollywood-style stucco mansion with sunken swimming pool? Do you yearn for a small fairy-tale cottage draped in ivy? Or do you both covet an Arts and Crafts–style bungalow with a big backyard? Make lists of the qualities of your ideal home, and be as specific as you like. It's a great springboard to a discussion on your future plans as a couple.

CITY, SUBURBS, OR COUNTRY — OH MY!

Unless it's a foregone conclusion that your new nest will be in a particular location, this is something you need to discuss as a couple. If one of you is a "city mouse" and the other a "country mouse," perhaps you can agree on something in between—such as a peaceful suburb with an easy commute to town. If he loves the urban environment and you long for a rustic country retreat nearby a lake, be creative. Could you live in the city and put money aside for a weekend place? Could living more cheaply in the suburbs or countryside allow for a weekend per month at a fancy hotel in the city? Or, could you agree on a timeline that suits your lifestyle—say, the next few years in the city, followed by a move to someplace quieter when you're ready to start a family?

The City

PROS	CONS
✓ Entertainment and cultural events	✗ Expense (including insurance and other hidden costs)
✓ Restaurants and bars	✗ Crime
✓ Sense of fun and excitement	✗ Litter
✓ Diversity of experiences and people	✗ Less family-friendly
✓ Public transportation, easily walkable	✗ Limited space
✓ Historical points of interest	✗ Noise
	✗ Few green spots

The Burbs

PROS	CONS
☑ Less expensive	☒ Can be bland and dull
☑ Quiet and serene	☒ Feeling of isolation
☑ Safe	☒ Less diversity, vibrancy
☑ Sense of community	☒ Family-oriented (only a con if you don't have kids)
☑ Ease of lifestyle	☒ More drive time
☑ Clean, new housing	☒ Fewer cultural or historical points of interest
☑ Spacious	

THE BOUDOIR AND BEYOND

If you've been living on your own for a long while, it may be a shock to have a man in your bedroom every night and every morning. While it can take some getting used to the piles of clothes he leaves at the foot of the bed, or the gym shoes, or the sports magazines stacked on the nightstand, the truth is the bedroom now belongs to both of you—and it should feel like it. Fill the bedroom with the colors and smells you both enjoy; keep electronics and work items out of sight; and use the bedroom for only two things: sleeping and lovemaking. By treating the bedroom as a romantic retreat for the two of you at the end of the day, you'll likely see him regard it this way, too.

The Ideal Bedroom

CHECKLIST

- ✓ The bed should be positioned so that there's plenty of room on each side— remember, there's not just one person climbing in anymore.

- ✓ Splurge on wonderful sheets in a color scheme you both like, plus plenty of pillows. (Chances are, he's never experienced the joy of 400-thread-count sheets—and he may never want the two of you to get out of bed!)

- ✓ Curtains can add a lot of romance to the room. Try long, romantic sheers in a warm color, topped by heavy velvet drapes for sleeping in on Sundays.

- ✓ Create a space on the bedside table for romantic accoutrements: set out a sandalwood candle (flowery scents can be overbearing for men), a romantic massage oil, and a lamp with a flattering, yellow- or pink-hued bulb.

continued on next page

The Ideal Bedroom

continued

- ✓ In your nightstand drawer so they're close at hand, stock your favorite sensual aids.

- ✓ Keep plenty of sexy CDs in the bedroom: Try jazz, our easy-listening chillout music.

- ✓ If you must keep office items in this room, store them in a cupboard or closed bin.

- ✓ Keep the walls of your room pale. You can easily add colour and personalize your space by selecting pictures and adding soft furnishings to your tastes—and these things are easy to change as time goes by.

- ✓ Make your room a telephone-free space. Leave your mobile phones out in the living room or better yet, turn them off when you come into the house.

- ✓ No television. Period. (If he argues, promise you'll provide better entertainment than it ever did.)

- ✓ No work. Period. Bringing work into the bedroom adds a stressful element to what should be an enjoyable, sensual, and peaceful environment. If you need a comfortable place to go through your paperwork or to work on your laptop, try the couch!

- ✓ Rid the room of overhead lighting. It's never flattering, and light switches are not often within easy reach of your bed.

- ✓ Add mirrors, and not for the reason you think. Reflective surfaces, coupled with soft lighting, will make your room glow.

- ✓ Keep a laundry hamper in the corner so you're not distracted during lovemaking by an unsightly heap of dirty clothes on the floor. Make it easy for your man to keep things tidy.

CREATING ROMANTIC RITUALS AT HOME

Once you've chosen a home and settled in together, it's surprisingly easy to slip into a routine. Don't fall into that trap! Even if everything is going swimmingly—or, some might say, *especially* if it is—you might start to take each other for granted. One way to combat this is to create weekly rituals that connect you as a couple, and that each of you can look forward to in the midst of your busy week. You'll be surprised how much these help to keep the romance fresh in your home.

Romantic Rituals

CHECKLIST

- ✓ Sunday morning breakfasting on Eggs Benedict and doing the crossword in your pajamas
- ✓ Friday night happy hour cocktails
- ✓ Making dinner together from a new recipe, one night per week
- ✓ Hosting a dinner party for close friends once a month
- ✓ Taking an evening stroll before bed
- ✓ Having a television-free night spent reading together or listening to a favorite CD
- ✓ Giving each other a back rub or foot massage at the end of the day
- ✓ An evening bath
- ✓ Gardening together on Saturday afternoons
- ✓ A weekend routine of picking up pastries at a favorite bakery
- ✓ Tuesday movie nights at home or the theater—alternate who gets to pick the flick

IT'S YOUR MONEY

Pooling your finances is one of the most intimate aspects of living together. Suddenly, you have to talk about details that you may never have divulged before to anyone—how much money you make, how much money you spend, and where your financial priorities lie. This is very personal stuff, but it's essential to establish early on some financial ground rules and expectations.

Begin by talking about what you think you can save as a couple each month, what you will spend, and where the money will go. Does he cringe at the idea of expensive shoes but believes in splurging on golf clubs? Do you want to save for exotic trips together, while he'd rather go camping and put the money in a retirement fund? These are the kinds of conversation you will need to have, either alone with your man or with the help of a financial advisor. Whether you decide to keep separate accounts, a joint account, or a combination of the two, you will be sharing expenses—and with that sharing comes not only intimacy, but also some tricky negotiation.

Like it or not, once you are sharing a home, you'll have to succumb to the "B" word. Yes, a budget. Don't think you can get away without one. Even if you keep your other income and expenses separate, make a list of all the household expenses you can think of, and decide the most equitable way to divide them. (Also take into account each person's financial picture, from who makes more money to who has more debt.) Then, chart out who pays what and when. By establishing this early, and ideally in writing, you'll avoid headaches and misunderstandings later. Too many couples have combusted because of arguments about money.

JOINT HOUSEHOLD EXPENSES

Indicate an estimated amount and whose responsibility it is to pay the bill: his, hers, or both.

Expense per month	Amount	His	Hers	Shared
Rent/mortgage		☐	☐	☑
Phone/cable		☐	☐	☑
Individual cell phones		☐	☐	☑
Electricity		☐	☐	☑
Gas		☐	☐	☑
Water		☐	☐	☑
Local taxes		☐	☐	☑
Vehicles		☑	☐	☐
Vehicle insurance		☐	☑	☐
Home contents insurance		☐	☑	☐
Groceries		☐	☑	☐
Household items/supplies/ furnishings		☑	☐	☐
Entertainment (movies, dinners out, etc.)		☑	☐	☐
Clothing/toiletries/ grooming		☐	☑	☐
Savings/investments		☑	☐	☐
Holidays		☐	☐	☑

ROOM TO BREATHE

While it may be tempting to spend *all* your time together when you're in the throes of brand-new cohabitation, remember to play it cool. You don't want to smother one another. And, if your man has had commitment issues in the past (and what man hasn't?), his head may already be spinning at the thought of his bachelor life ending for good. He might miss his time alone, or his time with the boys. If every time he turns around he sees you there, this panic will escalate. So remember the lessons you learned while dating: leave him wanting more.

Even though you've made a major commitment, you can retain a little mystery—and a life of your own. It will only make you more appealing. Make sure that you schedule nights out with the girls, or even short vacations to see friends or family without him. Let him have a free afternoon while you're out shopping, and then surprise him with a little treat when you get home. Take a class or volunteer one night a week. Just because you live together doesn't mean you have to be at each other's beck and call all the time. It's good for each of you to have a little breathing room, and the relationship will flourish because of it.

If possible, create separate spaces in your new home for each of you. Perhaps the garden is your domain, and the garage his. If you live in an apartment, is there a guest bedroom or even a corner of the living room where you can follow your own pursuits—even things as simple as knitting, drawing, or reading in a favorite chair? Set up those individual spaces as best you can; it's a reminder that you are still individuals. You will find that if you agree to your man turning the guest room into a gym or the garage into a sculpting studio, you may get back more than you give up. He will have a place to retreat—and those breathers will only make him happier to see you when you come together again.

Plus, he'll appreciate your independence and your consideration of his needs more than you know.

There are other benefits to creating separate spaces. If you happen to be more than a bit obsessive-compulsive, know that you'll have one room over which you rule. You can decorate it, arrange it, clean it, and occupy it as you wish. Conversely, he can fill his space with as many power tools as he wants, however messy they are. But you must both agree to respect your respective domains. If you create a quilting room, he can't rummage around when he needs a tape measure. He must ask you to enter. And resist that urge to straighten up his room. While his space might seem to lack rhyme or reason at first blush, he certainly has his own "method" of organization and "style" of decor. Leave him be. And when the very idea of his grubby music studio becomes over-whelming, head to your meditation room, light a candle, and be thankful that you have a private sanctuary to retreat to.

STAYING

ON THE

SAME PLANET

In this chapter, you'll learn how to:

✳ Embrace that silly "sports thing" of his ✳ Get him to take an interest in your pastime ✳ Make him feel more manly ✳ Fix his favorite meals and get him to love yours ✳ Create different chores for both of you ✳ Keep the house tidy when he is not

ONCE YOU BEGIN THE DELICATE ART OF COHABITATION, YOU may find it, shall we say, *challenging*, to merge your worlds—your belongings, interests, opinions, hobbies, and professional aspirations. It may at first blush seem inconceivable to set your antique crystal lamp next to his wagon-wheel coffee table, let alone talk to him about your interest in soapmaking or his passion for hockey. But don't fret! With a strong constitution and more than a bit of crafty compromise, you can be both interested in and interesting to each other.

HAVE A HOBBY . . .

In looking at many successful relationships, it's obvious the key to happiness and longevity is to pursue separate interests and hobbies. As much as you love that man of yours, it's unrealistic and a tad unreasonable to spend every hour of every day with him. Forget about how trapped he will feel for just a minute. Take a rare moment to think first about yourself.

What do you love to do? Bake fancy cakes? Read juicy historical romances? Garden? Shop with your girlfriends? Volunteer? Go for long runs? Now imagine your man joining you for every activity. Imagine him discussing politics with you as you are trying to follow the directions of a complicated soufflé. Can you picture him tagging along as you try on dresses with your friends? While he may come in handy when you want someone to carry your bags, resist the urge to include him in your activities. You need time to maintain your interests and spread your wings. In doing so, you will feel more challenged and engaged. You will be able to bring skills into the home and you'll be able to pepper your conversations with exciting information and insight.

Now let's think about your relationship and your man. Spending every waking moment with him will more likely evoke feelings of obligation and resentment, not love and intimacy. Do not confuse quality with quantity. The amount of time you spend with your man is not a measure of how healthy or blissful your union is.

If you've been focused on creating a home for you and your man, spend a bit of time focusing on yourself and what you might like to do. Take a class or join an organization to get yourself out of the house and mingling with other folks. Even starting a monthly reading group with a few friends can spark your intellect and prevent you from going stir crazy. You can only redecorate the guest bathroom so many times!

. . . AND TAKE AN INTEREST IN HIS!

There's no way to put this gently. Sports matter to him . . . and therefore they matter to you. So take a little time to learn about various sporting events so you can talk intelligently about his favorite team and even join him as an armchair fan.

The first step in embracing his zeal for sports is to respect his interest and level of enthusiasm. Do not scoff at it as a waste of time and money. Save questions until a commercial break. If you pester him, he will ignore you or even snap at you. Don't take it personally. Just learn from the first time and wait for a lull to chat. If you haven't been watching the game with him, you won't know if you are interrupting him during a critical moment. You certainly wouldn't want him to interrupt you when the best actress award is being presented during the awards show you've been waiting all year to watch!

Now that you've dipped your toe into his sport, study the game. Get to know a few players on his team. You'll begin to perk up when they are playing or do something particularly well. You'll actually start rooting for them and the team. Study the recap of the game in the newspaper to familiarize yourself with the team's standing and player's statistics. Wear a cap or jersey every time his/your team is playing. Declare it's your lucky hat and you're too superstitious not to wear it. He will declare his eternal love to his team and to you!

If he likes outdoor pursuits, be it golf or mowing the lawn, praise him! Stroke his ego or give him a small token when he shoots a great 18 holes or mows the front lawn into a new checkerboard design. He will appreciate that you accept and even encourage his passion without feeling the need to join in. Of course, he'd probably be delighted if you wanted him to teach you a few things!

When it comes to sharing your interests with him, take it slow. Ease him into your hobby. If you enjoy a particular craft, make him something. Ask him questions; don't assume he'll like something because you like it. If you just read a particularly absorbing biography, tell him about a few details of the person's life that you know he'd find fascinating. If he doesn't take an interest right away, don't push it. Just embrace your own life and keep it as something private for yourself.

Sports: A Primer

SPORT	PLAYERS	HOW TO SCORE	PERIODS
Football	11 offensive, 11 defensive	Touchdown = 6 pts After TD kick = 1 pt After TD conversion = 2 pts in college; 1 in pro Field goal = 3 pts Safety = 2 pts	4 quarters
Basketball	5	Basket = 2 pts Basket beyond perimeter = 3 pts Free throws = 1 pt	2 halves in college; 4 quarters in pro
Baseball	9 on field	Run = 1 pt	9 innings
Hockey	6	Goal = 1 pt	3 periods
Soccer	11	Goal = 1 pt	2 halves
Golf	1 or more	The lowest total score wins	usually 18 holes
Rugby	15	Try = 5 pts Conversion kick = 2 pt Penalty goal = 3 pts Drop goal = 3 pts	2 periods
Boxing	2	Outright win for knockouts, otherwise points given out of 10 for particular blows	3 rounds

LOVE HIS FOOD

Better yet, learn to make his favorite dishes.

Pay attention to what he takes seconds of. When you are at a restaurant, notice what he tends to order. Does he love fish or is he a hard-core carnivore? Ask his mother what his favorite dishes from childhood are. Or take the next step and ask her to share the recipes with you. She'll love that, and your man will love your meatloaf.

But don't feel tied to making traditional dishes. A bit of experimentation will keep your cuisine—and relationship—zesty. Try making a different ethnic cuisine each week. If he loves Chinese food, find some takeout boxes at a party store and surprise him with his favorite homemade stir-fry packed in the box. Substitute your own fortunes into store-bought fortune cookies. See what he gobbles up. You'll be able to tell immediately if he *doesn't* like a dish, but sometimes men are less forthcoming when they *do* like something. Ask. You might be surprised which dish he's remembering with relish.

But, for goodness sake, you don't have to slave over a hot stove every night! Take the night off now and again. Order out. Keep takeout menus handy and highlight which dishes you both liked. Agree to order one new dish to share and sample every time you order out.

If he hates what you love, all is not lost. There are ways to work around the problem. Naturally, you can order your favorite foods when you are out with your girlfriends. If you don't eat red meat (or any kind of meat, for that matter), develop a few pasta dishes or casseroles where the meat is on the side or nonexistent. He may be surprised how easy it is to forgo meat. With careful planning, he may not even notice the omission at all! Swap spinach for spicy sausage in your lasagna and check his reaction, if he has one at all. Make baked beans and leave out the bacon. He will never miss that smoky pork product.

FAIL-SAFE LASAGNA

This is my mother's lasagna recipe and it is the way to any man's undying affection. I've received offers of marriage due to this recipe. And it's a snap. Don't sniff at the cottage cheese; it's key to achieving a perfect balance of textures and flavors. And if you want a vegetarian option, simply fold into the cheese mixture a drained box of frozen chopped spinach and forgo the sausage. *Serves 6 to 8.*

You will need	**WHAT TO DO**
1 lb spicy Italian sausage	**1** Preheat the oven to 350°F (180°C).
1 onion, chopped	**2** Brown the sausage (remove from casings, if necessary) with the onion and garlic in a skillet. Drain the oil and then transfer the sausage mixture to a large saucepan. Add the spaghetti sauce.
2 cloves garlic, minced or pressed	
1 x 26-oz jar and 1 x 14-oz jar spaghetti sauce	**3** In a bowl, mix together $1^3/4$ cups of the mozzarella with the cottage cheese and milk. Reserve the remaining mozzarella to sprinkle on top of the lasagna.
2 cups shredded mozzarella cheese	**4** Grease a 9 x 13-inch lasagna or cake pan.
16 oz cottage cheese	**5** To assemble the lasagna: First, spread 1 cup of the sauce on the bottom of the pan, then a layer of pasta, then another 1 cup of sauce, $1^1/2$ cups of cheese sauce, a second layer of pasta, 1 cup of sauce, and $1^1/2$ cups of cheese sauce. Sprinkle the reserved mozzarella on top.
1/4 cup milk	
8 oz (1/2 box) dried lasagna sheets	
	6 Cover with aluminum foil. Bake for 30 minutes. Remove foil and bake for additional 30 minutes, or until the cheese topping has browned.
	7 Serve hot, accompanied by a green salad.

PORK CHOPS WITH CORN DRESSING

Before you wrinkle your nose at a recipe that calls for cream corn, try it out. The corn dressing provides a delicious, innovative complement to the succulent pork chops. *Serves 4.*

You will need	WHAT TO DO
6–8 pork chops, thinly cut	**1** Preheat the oven to 350°F (180°C).
¼ cup mustard	**2** Baste the chops with the mustard, salt, and pepper. In a frying pan, brown both sides in oil. Remove the chops and place in a baking dish.
salt	
pepper	**3** Pour the grease out of the skillet. Add 1 cup of water to the skillet and boil.
4 tablespoons vegetable oil	**4** Mix the cream corn, corn kernels, egg, and bread in a separate dish. Pour the mixture over the pork chops. Pour the liquid from the skillet over the chops and corn mixture.
1 x 16 oz can cream corn	
1 x 16 oz can whole corn kernels	**5** Cover with aluminum foil and bake for 45 minutes. Remove the foil and bake for 15 minutes, or until the top is nicely browned.
1 egg	
2–3 slices white bread, shredded	

PERFECT POT ROAST

This dish sent me over the moon when I was a kid and I still swoon when my mother, the ultimate homemaker, serves this up for me or her man. *Serves 4 to 6.*

You will need		**WHAT TO DO**
5 lb round bone or English blade roast	**1**	Preheat the oven to 350°F (180°C).
2 tablespoons flour	**2**	Flour, salt, and pepper each side of the roast.
salt	**3**	In a roasting pan (or a 9 x 12-in cake pan), brown the roast over medium heat.
pepper	**4**	Add the onion, carrots, mushrooms, and 1 1/2 cups water to the pan.
1 large onion, thickly sliced	**5**	Cover the pot and cook for 1 1/2 hours. The meat should almost fall apart at this point.
2 cups carrots, thickly sliced or whole	**6**	Serve hot, accompanied by mashed potatoes with gravy. To make gravy, mix 1/2 cup of cold water and 2 tablespoons of flour together to make a thick paste. Add to the roast drippings (still in the roast pan) over low heat and stir constantly until the gravy thickens. If it becomes too thick, simply add more water.
2 cups mushrooms, whole		

DON'T MAKE A DRAMA
OUT OF DUTY

You have probably heard it before. Your girlfriend's guy forgot to take out the trash . . . again. This is understandably irritating, but don't you dare throw in the towel and accept defeat!

Revert to a few childish tactics. Offer your man-boy special prizes, incentives, or even an allowance each week for jobs well done. Present him with coupons instead of cash when he earns his keep.

When first setting up house, split the chores. You could even post a list on the refrigerator or another trafficked area. He won't fail to notice when he's not pulling his weight.

Don't let things fester. Write down your peeves on a slip of paper and flush it down the toilet. But don't jump on him if you've been stewing all day because he forgot to take out the trash . . . again. Give him a chance to unwind and maybe remember on his own. Cut him a wide berth for an hour or so, and spend that time doing something for yourself—take a bath. If he continues to forget, help him remember. Leave him casual notes. Don't wait for him to slip up. Give him positive reinforcement when he remembers. Gratuitous praise, a kiss, or another form of appreciation will guarantee that he'll be taking out the trash a day early.

Sigh . . . so what if you live with a slob? Sorry to say, you may have to accept his slovenly behavior but you don't have to live in a pigsty. Make it easy for him to be clean. Place bins around the bedroom and bathroom and lots of trashcans throughout the house. If you resent picking up after your man, give him other tasks that even out the work-load in your mind. Picking up the kids, handling the bills/checking accounts, and maintaining the cars can all help lessen your feeling of running a one-woman maid service.

MAKE HIM FEEL LIKE A MAN

Even if you wear dungarees or those darling capri pants now and again, let your man know that *he* wears the proverbial pants in your twosome. Cede manly household tasks, like repairing the roof or fixing a leaky faucet, to him. Why, he'll puff up like a blowfish if you ask him to do a simple task like check the air pressure on your tires! *You* know you can do these tasks, but why break a nail or a sweat when you have a perfectly good man in need of a little ego stroking? When he heads to the garage with a tire gauge, spend that time doing something much more palatable to you.

Let him feel as if he is the master of his domain. Carve out an area, be it the garage or the kitchen, where he is king. Let him organize and decorate it the way he wants. Let him rule in certain areas about which you don't care and ones at which he'll excel. These may be traditional male bastions like mechanics or landscaping, or he might shine in historically female arenas, such as sewing, gardening, or cooking. Hold your tongue if you dislike his taste. Just turn your attention to the other areas of your home.

When it comes to dressing, why not dress to accentuate *his* best features? Wear flats to accentuate his height. Slip into dresses and skirts to complement his inherent manliness. Spritz on a floral perfume and slick on a shimmery lipgloss. It's fun to be a girl, and he will admire your female form!

Of course, don't let it be suggested that you should sacrifice practicality for style. If you find yourself washing a car, you certainly shouldn't wear your best leather heels or togs that require drycleaning. Always dress for the occasion, but find a way to amplify your innate girlishness. Even adding a comely hair accessory to your coif can make walking the dog an opportunity to be admired.

DO	DON'T
✓ Wear lipstick or lipgloss	✗ Wear only Chapstik year-round
✓ Stock a manly scented soap in the shower	✗ Fill the medicine cabinet with feminine products
✓ Wear ballet flats	✗ Wear heels if you will tower over him
✓ Wear a pretty nightgown	✗ Wear his old T-shirt to bed
✓ Surrender the garage to him	✗ Feng shui his toolbox
✓ Have shiny, touchable hair	✗ Overload your hair with stiff gels and hairspray
✓ Dress for the occasion	✗ Wear clothes that restrict movement
✓ Ask for his opinion when dressing for a night out	✗ Wear a getup you know he hates
✓ Ask him what scents he likes	✗ Light floral candles or place potpourri in the bathroom
✓ Tuck a fresh flower behind an ear	✗ Make a habit out of complicated updos
✓ Keep a lacy shawl handy for chilly nights	✗ Tie an old sweatshirt around your waist
✓ Protect your delicate complexion with SPF	✗ Nag him about his skincare regime
✓ Wear colors that complement his complexion	✗ Wear hues he hates
✓ Highlight your décolletage with a delicate pendant	✗ Wear revealing tops that attract the attention of strangers
✓ Wear clothes that fit your body	✗ Hide your figure under shapeless tents
✓ Buff his nails	✗ Ask him to moisturize or exfoliate

THE LOST ART OF

DOMESTIC

DIPLOMACY

In this chapter, you'll learn how to:

✳ Master the delicate art of negotiation ✳ Train him
to take on and remember tasks and chores ✳ Develop strategies
for "mister meanors" ✳ Calm down before you blow up
✳ Communicate effectively to get your way

YOU'RE IN LOVE. THINGS ARE GREAT. WHY TALK, LET ALONE *think*, about the ways that he irritates you? Well, in this case it pays to map out a few strategies to deal with domestic drama.

There are going to be little things that he does or doesn't do that are going to irk you. And your first instinct is to give him a piece of your mind. It's okay to *feel* that way. It's natural, it's right, it's good. What isn't such a good idea is acting rashly on that feeling. It isn't prudent. So where does that leave you?

AVOID BEING A NAGGER

Many women channel their frustration by vigorously throwing themselves into housework. They give their man the silent treatment while they scrub the grout in the bathtub. Ladies, repeat after me: He can't read minds! If you are peeved that he didn't remember to wash the car or pick up the drycleaning, don't expect him to figure out his memory lapse on his own. If you're in a bad mood, he'll just chalk it up to "women's issues." And that will just enrage you further, driving his point home that your hormones are raging.

Stop. Take a deep breath. Pretend someone is zipping you into a really tight-fitting dress and hold it. Slowly release this. Do this as many times as need be until adrenalin stops coursing through your body and your complexion has returned to its natural hue.

That's better. There are two courses of action: *preventative measure*s to make sure he doesn't bungle things again and *counter measures* to immediately address the situation.

PREVENTATIVE MEASURES

You don't want to be his mommy—he'll only rely on you more as time goes by, and a few years from now, you'll be making his dentist appointments for him and leaving him notes to brush his teeth. That's just not sexy. Agreeing to what are "his" jobs and "her" jobs will go a long way to ensure there is no confusion as to whose responsibility it is to take out the trash or empty the litter box. Make a list of the weekly chores and agree to whose is whose. Use reminders only for things out of the ordinary.

It goes without saying that your man should do his basic chores around the house as part of the partnership of living together. But when you want him to do "extra" things, like car maintenance, house painting, or chopping wood, use the old-fashioned barter system: Give him positive reinforcement when he does something you like (and avoids doing something you don't!). If he knows that he's working for something aside from domestic bliss, he may be additionally motivated. Explain that there is an expiration date on rewards to encourage him to complete the task in a timely fashion.

Use this handy chart as a general guideline but feel free to get creative in your reciprocation.

Positive Reinforcement

	HE...		YOU...
1	Paints the bathroom	1	Pay for the two of you to paint the town red
2	Does the taxes	2	Do the dishes for a month
3	Changes the oil	3	Bestow a special sexual favor
4	Fixes a clogged drain	4	Fix breakfast in bed
5	Washes the dog	5	Give him a sponge bath
6	Washes the car	6	Make his favorite dish
7	Cleans the gutters	7	Buy baseball tickets for him and his friends
8	Cleans out the garage	8	Clean out the closet
9	Rakes leaves	9	Caddy for him on 18 holes of golf
10	Gets the car(s) inspected	10	Give him the television for an entire Sunday

If your guy is forgetful and has a hard time remembering basic tasks, you can get him up to speed and then slowly wean him off your assistance. Post gentle reminders in a prominent location. Hang a dry erase board in a central location, such as the kitchen, with reminders for both of you so he doesn't feel singled out. Schedule things into his PDA if he's of the paperless persuasion. Many computers even offer the equivalent of yellow sticky notes on the desktop.

You may not think you should have to remind him of small or repetitive tasks but, my dear, you do. Ask him if he minds or needs the reminders and if he's appreciative, keep it up. After he has successfully performed a chore or errand with your help for a sustained period of time, try pulling back on your prompting for a week or two. Is he continuing to perform at the same level of excellence and reliability? If so, withdraw your help permanently . . . or until he starts slacking.

If his contribution around the house leaves something to be desired, make it a game. Challenge him on a Saturday. Split up your chores and see who finishes first. If one of his tasks involves cleaning the house or pulling weeds in the garden, set up a scavenger hunt. Tell him you've placed coins or bills around the living room or garden and they are his to keep if he finds them all while dusting or weeding.

This kind of stroking is bound to grate on your modern sensibilities, but if you want particular results, you have to be willing to think outside of the feminist box.

And you must be patient. Reconditioning takes time. Think about his upbringing. If he never learned to wash a dish properly, don't hold that against him. Just show him the correct way to do it.

Nagging isn't just about falling down on the job. Sometimes living together in a confined space can cause stress and irritation. To prevent this, give him space. The two of you do not have to spend every spare minute together. In fact, it's probably a bad idea if you do. (No matter how much you love someone, you will get sick of him eventually if you are joined at the hip.) If he wants to be alone for an hour or an afternoon, don't take it personally. He needs his breathing space, and if you allow him to hang out with his friends, tinker in the basement, or test-drive cars, he will return to you refreshed and eager for your company. Instead of focusing on why he doesn't want to be with you right then, take advantage of the time to putter yourself—be it shopping for vintage clothes, catching up with your girlfriends, planting bulbs, or watching old movies all afternoon in your pajamas. You'll forget all about him and be excited to tell him about your day when you reconnect.

Create a nag-free zone. Designate an area of your home where your guy can be as messy or uncouth as he wants to be. The basement is an ideal location to house all his college memorabilia and tragic experiments in interior design. Resist the temptation to clean it or supply the room with coasters.

COUNTER MEASURES

Choose your battles. Avoid chiding him for everything, both large and small. You will lose your impact if you cry wolf.

Plan ahead and do not lose your cool in the heat of the moment. If you notice a trend such as forgetfulness, messiness, or presumptuousness, group them together into a general discussion of how it makes you feel. Keep the focus on yourself. He can't argue with how you *feel*.

A well-crafted conversation:

"Honey, can I talk to you for a second?"

"Sure, sweetie."

"Well, I wanted to convey how agitated I get when I don't know that your friends are coming over to watch a game. You know how much

I like them but I feel unprepared and a bit, well, invaded when I didn't expect them."

"It's no big deal. They don't expect you to wait on them or feed them."

"I know. It's just that I can't help but be in hostess mode when your friends are here, and I'd feel less stressed if I knew in advance they were coming. It may seem silly but that's just me."

"Honey, I didn't know you felt that way. I'll make sure to let you know the day before or call you from work if I invite anyone over."

A less-successful attempt:

"Do you have any idea how rude it is not to tell me you invited people over? I live here too, or did you forget?"

"Geez, lighten up. Why do you have to make a federal case out of everything?"

"There you go again, trivializing the situation instead of taking responsibility for your lack of consideration."

"I'm taking a shower."

Do you see the difference? The first example features a woman who knows not to attack her man or his actions to get what she wants. Instead, she focuses on how his actions (or lack thereof) make her feel. No man wants to make his loved one feel bad on purpose. The second illustration shows a woman on the offensive, and no matter how right she is, her man is going to be unresponsive and defensive and cast her as a shrew. No man wants to be henpecked.

As tempting as it may be to avoid saying anything at all, do not suppress your feelings. You will blow your well-coiffed top if you let

everything that bothers you fall by the wayside. The truth is, nothing really falls by the wayside in your mind, does it? You remember every darn thing, which makes you great at your job and keeping house, but can also shut you down emotionally and turn you into a ticking bomb.

Be kind. You cannot have a conversation with your man about something you want him to change without raising his defensive shield. Even if he's clearly in the wrong about something, his first thought is fight or flight. You don't want him to do either, so what do you do? Well, avoid sarcastic comments or a superior attitude. Tell him that it's really important to you to create a home where both people are working toward a common goal and making each other happy. Make jokes where appropriate to keep the mood light.

Be creative. Your man will get the picture if you paint him one . . . literally. If you are upset about something and can't voice how you feel, write it down in a letter or even draw him a picture. If he continually forgets to water the garden, sketch a plot full of desiccated weeds, dead flowers, wilted leaves, and a sad-looking bee. If he forgets to lock the back door, write a comedic horror story about what would happen if a burglar came in and fingered his mother's heirloom silver. If these approaches seem just juvenile and passive-aggressive, well, they are. But visual aids are an excellent way to lead into a conversation with a bit of levity.

Do not retaliate. Know that your man isn't purposely disappointing you, so if he displays bad behavior or forgets a task, don't give him the silent treatment or a piece of your mind. And definitely do not forgo your own responsibilities to spite him. He will most likely not even notice!

If you lose your temper, all is not lost. Apologize and again bring the focus back to how you feel when he jokes about you in front of his friends or how agitated you get when the house isn't clean.

AVOID HITTING HIM

You are obviously a well-bred lady and would never hit someone, particularly the love of your life. So let's talk about the other kind of low blows you can inflict (i.e., hitting below the belt).

Your guy might love teasing you or sharing funny stories about you in front of your friends. Perhaps he's had a bit too much to drink and acts like a buffoon, ruining for you what would otherwise have been a lovely evening. This may, to put it delicately, rub you the wrong way. Whatever happens, you must resist the urge to give him a tongue-lashing or embarrass him in a similar fashion. Put away those baby photos of him in a dress! This will only escalate the situation and you will lose ground in the long run. Take the high road, turn the other cheek, and spend your time instead thinking of all the ways he can make it up to you. Now you get the picture.

As your mind drifts off, take deep breaths and imagine your anger or embarrassment ebbing away. If need be, go to the restroom and vent in private. There will be a time and place—when your guy will be most receptive (that is, not defensive)—to air your feelings. Think about the big picture. Your man loves you but is experiencing an unfortunate lack in judgment. This will pass.

So it goes without saying that you should not pout or sulk. He can't read your mind, even though you think he should be able to figure out your mood by your dour expression as soon as he walks through the door. There are healthier alternatives to inflicting permanent damage on him, your relationship, or his stuff.

Healthier Alternatives

	WHAT YOU WANT TO DO...		WHAT YOU SHOULD DO INSTEAD...
1	Release a video on the Web of him singing "The Crying Game"	1	Take him to karaoke, ply him with liquor, and have him perform in front of his chums
2	Remove the hood ornament on his luxury convertible	2	Drive his car through the mud
3	Pulverize the remote	3	Invite the girls over for a night of weepy chick flicks
4	Make a dish he's allergic to	4	Make your favorite dish
5	Wash his favorite wool sweater in hot water	5	Wear his favorite wool sweater—and nothing else—for a saucy surprise
6	Tell his pals about his sexual preferences	6	Make him perform all your favorite sexual preferences
7	List all of the stupid things he's ever said and send it out as a chain-letter e-mail	7	List all of the stupid things he's ever said in your journal

Forgiveness is a two-way street. If you are gracious and let his transgressions go quietly into the night, chances are that he'll respond in kind when you fall down on the job. It seems impossible to fathom, but there will come a day when you, too, are less than perfect.

HOW TO COMPROMISE

You may not like certain behavior or character traits of his, but you may have to accept that you are not always going to be simpatico. In fact, your goals, tastes, and habits might differ greatly. And to be sure, your goals will be more lofty, your taste more exquisite, and your habits more healthy. Even so, you have to meet him somewhere in the middle, if only to give him a hand to the promised land . . . of behavior modification.

HIGH CRIMES

Your man violates the laws of what is right and good more than he knows. Figure out what grievous offenses—fella nees—merit hard time and decide to let him get away with minor crimes—mister meanors.

Fella nees	Hard time
Frequently skips foreplay	Withhold sex until he holds you!
Lacks goals	Buy him sessions with a life coach for his birthday
Drinks too much	Videotape him every time he imbibes and put together a tape for his viewing displeasure
Smokes too much	Computer forecast how he'll look in 20 years if he continues to smoke
Dislikes your chums	Host a weekly girls' night in
Dislikes your mom	Invite her to stay for a long weekend of enforced quality time
Never lets you get a word in edgewise	Using a timer, give him 5 or 10 minutes to say his piece. After that, you have the floor

Mister meanors	Behavior modification
Hogs the remote	Designate one night where YOU own the television
Stingy regarding vacations, dinners out	Plan your own trips and outings without him
Works long hours and weekends	Meet for lunch dates
Picks his teeth	Leave toothpicks next to the remote
Messy	Set hampers and trashcans in key locations around the house
Smelly	Withhold sexual favors unless he bathes
Tells bad jokes	Place some comics and humor books in the bathroom so he can get some new material
Doesn't read	Create a tradition of reading the Sunday paper together
Obsessed with his electronic "toys"	Become obsessed with your own battery-operated "toys"
Hard-core jock	Join him for workouts if he joins you for yoga
Hard-core couch potato	Work out or do yoga in front of the television
Terrible taste in music	Turn your favorite alternative radio station on during drives, while cooking, or when reading the paper
Constantly analyzes your Myers-Briggs	Retaliate with horoscope or palm reading

TURN THE TABLES

For the more advanced young lady who would like to get her way but make her man think it is his doing, here are a few suggestions.

Psych 101

CHECKLIST

☑ Offer him two options, be it a dress, vacation, or dinner, with one clearly something he would never pick. He'll have no choice but to select the better option, which is exactly the thing you wanted all along.

☑ Keep your eye on the prize. While it may be hard to lose a battle (especially when you know you're in the right), keep focused on winning the war. If your guy knows which buttons to push, refuse to be goaded into a quarrel. Instead, remember that it's not as important to win an argument over whose turn it is to cook supper as it is to keep your blood pressure down and maintain a state of domestic bliss. Pull a frozen tray of lasagna out of the freezer. You'll be rewarded later.

☑ Flirt with him. You know which buttons of his to push to excite him. While he's in a heightened state of excitement, he may be more inclined to agree to your wishes.

☑ Strike a bargain. Make promises of future benefits. For instance, "If you'll go with me to my parents, I'll do that thing you like." You may already be planning to do it but he doesn't have to know that. Keeping the tone playful will prevent this tactic from smacking of blackmail and will hardly seem like a sacrifice on his part.

☑ Mention things you did for him in the past. Subtly remind him that your relationship—while wonderful—is a give-and-take and it's his turn to give.

KEEPING
THINGS
ZESTY

In this chapter, you'll learn how to:

✳ Keep yourself looking fetching ✳ Embrace shopping together
✳ Dress to impress for any occasion ✳ Accentuate your physical assets
✳ Stop the sizzle fizzling ✳ Keep him guessing ✳ Leave him wanting more

YOU'VE REELED IN THE MAN YOU LOVE. WELL DONE. BUT the work is far from over. In fact, it's only just begun. And I'm not talking about perfecting your pot roast. You, dear, are a work-in-progress. You must diligently maintain a basic grooming routine, both to keep him satisfied and to continue to become the most glamorous and beguiling woman in your—and his—acquaintance.

For some well-heeled ladies, continually dabbling in beauty and fashion is pure heaven . . . and for some unfortunate souls, it's pure torture. So let's start at the beginning and work from there.

MINIMUM MAINTENANCE

It's fortuitous if you have a wash-and-go haircut and streamlined morning routine. It's even better if you were born beautiful and always smell vaguely of roses. But let's assume both these things are rather unlikely and that you need to do some work to keep yourself looking fresh and fetching.

If your guy leaves the house before you do, send him off to work with an appealing image that he can't wait to rush home to. If you are still in bed, you will have the pink flush of sleep on you and will look breathtaking. However, your breath won't be equally alluring. Keep a mint or breath spray in your bedside table for a quick refresher before you kiss him goodbye. If you eat breakfast together before going your separate ways, at least run a comb through your hair, splash water on your face, brush your teeth, and swipe some clear or tinted lipgloss over your lips to soften them—and him—up.

Don't let yourself go, even if you are home alone. Of course, this is as important for yourself as much as for him. Keep your lips moisturized, preferably with a red or pink color that makes you happy, before you clean, cook, or do the bills. Slather your hands with lotion after washing the dishes. You'll feel as if you are pampering yourself, which will help stave off the inevitable self-pity that's bound to emerge when you are mopping the floor or making crème brûlée from scratch. You'll be a comforting vision when your man walks in at the end of a day.

Make time in your busy schedule for the trips to the hairdresser and beauty salon. Just because you've nabbed your man doesn't mean you don't still want to look your best for him. More importantly, you will be attractive to and cared for by the person who counts most—yourself.

BE GLAMOROUS, NOT GROSS

Resist the temptation to go overboard in keeping your man entranced. There's a fine line between fetching and foul, and while your guy might enjoy the occasional viewing of *Girls Gone Wild*, realize that this is only a vicarious thrill. He picked you to go to sleep and wake up with. He doesn't want to climb into bed, only to find a strange woman wearing a wig and the newest collection from Fredericks of Hollywood waiting to pounce.

That's not to say you can't ratchet up your va-va-voom! *Au contraire*. There are many clothing and behavior options available to the creative woman. Surprise him with the unexpected. Forgo your underpinnings and tell him about it during a dinner party or movie. Challenge him to a fierce game of strip Scrabble—every time one of you hits the double word score space, the other removes a piece of clothing. Introduce a new piece of lingerie in rotation and "unknowingly" flash him a bit of it. Less is more and there is much power to be had in the unexpected.

You can also experiment with different looks using cosmetics and skincare products. A red lip or black cat eye can transform you into a drama mama. An application of shimmer lotion all over your body will make you glow. Apply scent at all your pulse points, which include the ankles, back of the knees, inner elbows, neck, and wrists. Keep the fragrance light. As your skin heats up, it will release the scent to anyone in close proximity. Hopefully, that means him.

The bottom line is that you should find what style works for you and him, but don't become beholden to it. Falling into a rut will cause you to become complacent with your grooming and perhaps even your romantic life. Even the simple act of buying a lipstick in a new color can be profound: you will feel as if you are indulging yourself and he will feel as if you are a saucy minx.

Grooming Tips

CHECKLIST

- ☑ Emphasize either your eyes or lips, not both.

- ☑ Line lips with liner, apply lipstick, blot, reapply for maximum wear.

- ☑ A bit of shimmer cream on your brow and cheekbones gives you a radiant glow.

- ☑ Men do make passes at girls who wear funky glasses.

- ☑ A creamy blush applied to the apples of your cheeks gives you the same flush as a lengthy make-out session.

- ☑ A heavily powdered face is outré but a spot of powder on a shiny nose is never sniffed at.

- ☑ Apply SPF to your face every day. Look for a moisturizer or foundation with sun protection.

- ☑ Lipgloss is a magical product but wipe it off if you are close to kissing your man or close to a pillowcase. Opt for a creamy lip balm instead.

- ☑ Reapply your makeup in the ladies room or another discreet area.

- ☑ Avoid trendy makeup colors and techniques. Seek out cosmetics that bring out and enhance your unique beauty.

- ☑ Exfoliate your feet and legs regularly to remove dry skin and callouses.

- ☑ Keep your toes polished, even in the dead of winter.

- ☑ Keep your fingernails clean and trimmed to the same length.

- ☑ Keep nose hair, moustaches, and stray whiskers out of sight. Never speak of their existence.

LET HIM HELP YOU DRESS

This concept might be too much to digest at first. Your man can't even button his own shirt correctly, so how on earth would he be able to keep abreast of the latest fashions? Well, he won't. However, he knows what he likes on you and he knows which features of yours he adores. The first thing to do is to pay attention to what he compliments. Does he love anything that shows off your décolletage? Does he seem appreciative when you slip into sleek black outfits? Is there one gingham sundress that drives him nuts? Start from there and continue your fact-finding mission. If you don't want to open the door for critical comments, ask his opinion about how various actresses or celebrities look on television or in magazines. You'll get a better idea of his taste and can shop accordingly.

If your constitution is strong, take him shopping. Keep it short! His attention span is built for sports matches not outlet malls. Bring him along to your favorite boutique or department store. Pick out a few things you like and see if he approves. Ask him to select a few things for you as well. Don't turn up your nose if he pulls out a taffeta creation with a keyhole opening or a leather-trimmed miniskirt. Hide your chagrin and gamely try it on for him. Wait for him to give his opinion and then explain why you feel uncomfortable wearing it. No matter how much he loves you in a black catsuit, he's not going to want you to wear something you feel indecorous or dowdy or just plain *wrong* in. At least we hope not.

A plea to the lady in you: Never wear your underwear as a visible accessory. Less is more—giving your guy a sneak peek is much more beguiling than exposing your skimpy panties over the waistband of your low-rise blue jeans.

If you like your	Wear
Ample bosom	V-neck blouses
Small bosom	A defined bodice, such as a delicate empire-waist top
Toned arms	$3/4$-length sleeves, halter tops
Flat stomach	Low-rise waistbands, snug knit tops
Boyish hips	A-line skirts
Tiny bottom	Form-fitting trousers or jeans
Hourglass figure	Pencil-line skirts, fitted sheath dresses
Petite frame	Skirts and dresses that hit above the knee
Slim legs	Short but not-too-short skirt
Slim waist	Fitted dresses and coats with belts

If you don't care for your	Wear
Thick arms	Long sleeves
Belly	High-waisted dresses or tunic tops
Big bottom	Long-flowing skirts
Child-bearing hips	Flat-front trousers with no pockets
Thick thighs	Generous cut trousers
Ample bosom	Round-necked tops in dark colors
Small bosom	Bosom-enhancing bras and tops

HIGH-MAINTENANCE MAGIC

If you are already well-groomed and well-dressed at all times, this may be preaching to the converted. However, there are a few tricks to ensure you are always well turned out for any occasion, in or out of the home. He will certainly not take you for granted and you'll always feel like a thoroughbred at the top of her game.

Keep a lipstick in each of your handbags, in the glove compartment of your car, and in each room of the house. You will never be caught off-guard with dry lips or a wan complexion. A colorful lipstick will give you a polished look, no matter how bare the rest of your face. If you are hosting a dinner party, during a trip to the kitchen, pull your lipstick out of the spice rack and freshen up between courses. Use the back of a spoon to check your application. During a backyard barbecue, pull out a shimmery lipgloss from the windowbox and discreetly swipe some on. While a mirror is not necessary for applying, you can use the reflective surface of the window glass. While watching the big game on TV with his chums, pull out your cosmetic aids from under a seat cushion and use as necessary to remain fresh as a daisy!

Get regular makeovers at your favorite department store. Keep up on the newest looks and rotate an alluring new eye shadow or cream blush into your collection. Do not submit to a whole trend look, however. Just incorporate one fresh look into your makeup kit. Makeup should always bring out your unique beauty, and your face should not be a canvas to the makeup movement *du jour*.

While your jewelry box should contain no more than heirloom pieces, you will want a few reliable items for your everyday signature look. Carefully select a pair of small earrings, ring, and/or pendant to show that, even running to the grocery store or going to an athletic event, you are perfectly dressed.

The occasion	Dress to impress
Baseball game	Jeans, sneakers, and a snug sweater
Charity black-tie gala	A gorgeous dress, of course; consider a pair of long gloves for old-school glamour
Holiday party at his company	Cashmere sweater in your most becoming color and a swingy skirt
Running errands	Capri pants, espadrilles, striped sailor shirt
Dinner at home	Wide-legged trousers and low-heeled mules—resist the urge to be casual!
Dinner and a movie	Colorful sweater set and jean skirt

When in doubt, overdress. It's always better to be overdressed for an occasion than underdressed. And keep your little black dress clean and at the ready, should an impromptu dinner or cocktail party invitation be extended.

It takes work to keep you looking your best, and when you first started dating your guy, you never let him see your efforts. But now that you're living together, it's not such a bad idea to let him in on the time, effort, and expense required to keep you in peak condition. If he has no inkling of how much money you spend on clothes and grooming, you may find yourself forced to conceal your spending habits and even blur the truth.

Many women do find it necessary to hide shopping bags in the trunk of the car until they can guarantee safe passage into the house. While this isn't advisable, if you do purchase a "spendy" item and don't want your guy to know the details of the sale, there are a few things you can do.

CHECKLIST

☑ Remove all tags and bags for your booty from the premises.

☑ Mix the item(s) into your other clothes or accessories in your closet.

☑ Casually wear the item and do not call attention to the fact that it's new.

☑ If asked if it is new, you have a few options. Truthful: "I've had it in the closet but this is the first time I'm wearing it. Do you like it?" Fictitious: "Yes, isn't it great? Jeanette bought it but decided she didn't like it and couldn't return it so she gave it to me."

☑ If asked if it was expensive, you also have a few routes to take. Truthful: "It was a bit pricey, but I've been working really hard and had some money saved up." Fictitious: "Gosh no. It was on the clearance rack at the outlet mall!"

CLOSE THE CURTAINS:
THE SEX FACTOR

If you've got this topic well in hand, bravo. That's wonderful news. However, your sex drive and his sex drive will speed and slow down at different times. With stress, change, hectic schedules, and biorhythms cropping up, it is to be expected that you won't be cruising along on the freeway of love without a pothole or two.

And routine can be a bit of a problem. You most likely know the benefit of spontaneity and innovation in your sex life, but you may be out of ideas. Do you feel as if the mystery is gone from your relationship every time he walks in on you while you're taking a bath? Does he hog the bed?

Take action before the sizzle fizzles.

Admittedly, it's radical, but open your mind to the idea of separation.

This isn't about a *legal* separation. Rather, why not consider creating separate spaces in your home that can serve as a recharge station or safe haven when you need some time to yourself? If you have the luxury, designate "his" and "her" bathrooms so your various unguents can be kept hidden. Set up a guest room that can serve as a second bedroom if one of you is sick, sleeping fitfully, working late, or just needs to take over all of the mattress real estate. Reassure your guy that you think this is healthy and is intended to keep an element of freshness and unpredictability in your relationship. You could even set up permanent separate bedrooms. There are no set rules to cohabitation. The important thing is that it feels right to the two of you; if fostering mystique and desire means separate beds or bedrooms, so be it. Some women even like to keep separate residences. It's not unheard of.

ASK HIM WHAT HE LIKES

It may feel awkward to outright ask him about his sexual preferences. If you are shy about this, look for other clues, such as groaning and heavy breathing, during sex. This indicates a high level of arousal, which in turn indicates that he likes what you're doing. If he holds you in place, continue what you're doing. If he gives you verbal cues or encouragement, stay the course. On the other hand, if he's unresponsive, quiet, and calm, you may want to switch gears.

If you are unable to decipher his body language or guttural noises, it's time to gather concrete information directly from the source. There are ways to ask him questions without seeming crude or indelicate. Here are a few to get you started. Do not interrogate him in one long session; you may overwhelm him. Instead, focus on one or two questions when he is relaxed or his guard is down.

CHECKLIST

- [x] What is your favorite position during sex?
- [x] What has been your most memorable sexual experience with me?
- [x] Is there anything I can do differently?
- [x] Do you think we have sex frequently enough? How often would you ideally like to have sex?
- [x] What are your thoughts on kissing? Foreplay? Oral sex?
- [x] What do you fantasize about?
- [x] What arouses you?

KEEP HIM GUESSING

Make an effort to change things every now and again. You don't want him to take you—and your needs—for granted. If there is one position you revere above all others, be careful not to direct him into it every time you have sex. Similarly, don't get stuck in a rut over the time of day you have sex or the frequency in which you engage in the pleasure principle.

If you love foreplay, try skipping it sometime and letting your primal urges take over. If you like morning sex, bring him breakfast in bed and spend the evening frolicking between the sheets.

CHECKLIST

- ☑ Serve him dessert in an apron . . . and nothing else.
- ☑ Put a special note in his fortune cookie or under his slice of cake.
- ☑ Challenge him to a game of strip poker.
- ☑ Give him a long, lingering sponge bath or join him in the shower.
- ☑ Wake him up with soft kisses.
- ☑ Strip-tease him.
- ☑ Leave a thank-you note for the previous evening in his briefcase.
- ☑ Place some goodies from the local sex shop in the medicine cabinet or night table. Wait for him to bring them up.
- ☑ Get fresh at the breakfast table.

Keep him in a perpetual state of anticipation over your next racy move. It doesn't matter what you do; the important thing is that you try something new from time to time. You may inspire your guy to return the favor!

BE DISCREET

Not to be a prude but a few things: Be discreet in front of your neighbors. Don't let your dirty laundry or dirty secrets hang out for all the world to see. It may seem thrilling at first, but when a neighbor gives you a long, knowing look in line at the deli, you may regret your indiscretion.

Be careful around the kids. While healthy displays of affection should be encouraged throughout the entire family, engage in more amorous activities behind closed (and locked) doors. What may seem right and natural in the heat of the moment may end up scarring your child for life and costing thousands in therapy.

It goes without saying but let's drive home the point anyway. Do not videotape or photograph yourself in compromising positions. Search for other, less permanent, ways to spice things up.

FRIENDS

AND

FAMILY:

THE CIRCLE OF LOVE

In this chapter, you'll learn how to:

✳ Maintain friendships with women and men
✳ Cope with friends and a partner who don't like each other
✳ Be prepared for any impromptu visit ✳ Host parties with grace
and flair ✳ Keep the in-laws happy—and at bay

NOW THAT YOU'RE ENJOYING A STATE OF DOMESTIC BLISS, it's shockingly easy to become lax in maintaining relationships outside the home. Resist the urge to make your man the center of your world. Even if you want to stay in with your guy and watch Hitchcock films, drag yourself off the couch once in a while and visit with friends and family. Stay in touch via phone if you must, but keep your relationships fresh and up-to-date.

After all, you never know when you'll need to call on them for support or, conversely, be there for a loved one in distress. While your man may seem to complete you, he probably hasn't known you since birth like your mother. He is most likely incapable of tactfully telling you that purple just isn't your color when you make a fashion mistake. And he certainly doesn't want to be your sounding board when you are not happy with him.

Cultivating your friendships is not just important for support and honesty. Making new friends and developing longtime relationships is essential for growth. Sharing different views and experiences, exploring ideas and issues, and finding safe haven to be yourself (let alone discover yourself) will guarantee that you stay an educated and insightful woman who you like, not to mention who your guy finds endlessly fascinating.

But beware. Know which friends are capable of full disclosure and with whom it is prudent to withhold specifics. Your pals and family love you and want the best for you. If they hear that you have isolated or ongoing issues with your man, they may not be completely supportive of your relationship. And if you are crazy in love, tread lightly as well. Not everyone is ecstatic with their romantic status—you may unintentionally rub salt in their wounds if you wax poetic about love, life, and your perfect man. Smugness is not a virtue!

KEEPING A LIFE
OUTSIDE THE HOME

It's of the utmost importance to sustain interests outside of your relationship. Value yourself and your career. You may be willing to give it up, but don't. You will come to welcome the opportunity to keep your intellect sharp and interests engaged. You will also be surrounded by motivated people with similar fields of interest.

In addition to drawing a paycheck for your skill and hard work, develop a few traditions or seek new adventures, such as:

CHECKLIST

- [x] Set a monthly girls' night out to catch up with your pals, or meet a friend once a week for a mani/pedi/gossip session.

- [x] Take a class in something completely new, with your man, a friend, or a group of strangers.

- [x] Keep up with your profession by attending a seminar or workshop.

- [x] Rather than always eating at the dinner table, pack a picnic when the weather's nice and head to the park or even your backyard.

- [x] Go hiking once a month with like-minded friends.

- [x] Take tennis lessons.

- [x] Prioritize travel options and commit to one trip a year.

- [x] Avoid going stir-crazy and get some fresh air. If you are doing something inside, ask yourself if you can take it outdoors. Yoga, reading, listening to music, talking with friends, and knitting can all be done under a tree.

- [x] Go to events in your town, even things you don't normally do—like art openings, book readings, concerts, etc. Just one conversation with an interesting stranger can totally energize you.

LOOSE LIPS SINK RELATIONSHIPS

You were probably close with girlfriends long before your beloved entered the picture. You have a storied history together and they know all your secrets.

This cannot continue.

There are pros and cons to sharing your dirty laundry with friends. They know your relationship baggage, are familiar with your foibles, and love you anyway. On the other hand, they are all too ready to think the worst of your guy if you offhandedly mention a thoughtless comment he said as he was running out the door.

As the old adage goes, knowledge is power, and controlling the flow of your relationship information allows you to retain some modicum of personal power. Your friends will want details. They will initially be taken aback by your media blackout. Kindly explain to them that as tempting as it is to divulge juicy details, you'd like them to help you be discreet and respectful of your man and your relationship. You can tell them that it's just not fair to share, and that you will always come to them if there's a real problem.

There's another reason to keep certain subjects to yourself, especially if things are going really well for you. Your friends may be single, and discussing domestic bliss may bring their relationship status into high relief. After a brunch spent discussing how your guy surprised you with a weekend trip to the shore, your friends may feel dispirited or acutely lonely. Be sensitive to their feelings and lead the conversation toward other equally engaging subjects.

What to share . . .

- ☑ your struggles to merge households
- ☑ your feelings about his family (and theirs toward you)
- ☑ friends of his you think would be a good match for a friend of yours
- ☑ his sweet gestures
- ☑ his questionable taste
- ☑ his funny quirks or comments
- ☑ your broad hopes for the future
- ☑ your new routines together

What to keep to yourself . . .

- ☑ details from the bedroom
- ☑ his "measurements"
- ☑ irritations, both major and minor, about your relationship
- ☑ a blow-by-blow account of your last tiff
- ☑ secrets he has shared with you
- ☑ your jealousy of his previous girlfriends
- ☑ any negative feelings he has about your friends
- ☑ how insanely happy you are not to be single

YOUR MAN AND YOUR FRIENDS

As difficult as it may be to accept, there will be times when your man and your friends won't get along. This is bound to happen with one or several of your friends. But recognize that, regardless of what they dislike about each other, *you* are their common denominator. While they love you and want what's best for you, they also may feel as if they are competing for your affection and time.

So it's up to you to make sure everyone feels loved and appreciated. Now that you are living with your man, it is more difficult to find time for all the people in your life. There's just not enough of you to go around. So you need to focus on quality, not quantity. Show your friends how much you value them by corresponding regularly by e-mail and calling them, even if you only have a few minutes. Drop them a handwritten note if you haven't seen them in some time. They will know that you're thinking of them, even if your schedule doesn't allow a get-together.

Avoid going too far in the other direction. Be cautious when scheduling too many activities with your friends. Your beloved might start to think you are unhappy or would rather be with your friends than him.

Do not try to bully anyone into liking each other. Don't make it your mission to campaign for your man or your friends. This could backfire. Providing details of someone's life or personality could give a friend or lover additional fodder to dislike the person, since he or she is already predisposed to skew any information in a negative way. And your man and friends want to make up their own minds, not feel as if they are being force-fed an unpleasant diet that you prescribe.

There will be times when your guy and your chums cross paths. When they do, find a shared interest for them to discuss. No matter how different your man and friends may be, there has to be something in which they are both interested. If you know they love the hometown sports team, bring them together to watch a game. If they like to try exotic food, meet up at a sushi bar or new Indian restaurant. It may be as simple as just mentioning a common interest when you are in their company. Who knows? This thoughtfulness on your part could be the ticket for them to see each other in a positive light. If this happens, take it slow. Don't be so encouraged that you think all bad feelings have been erased.

Know when to throw in the towel. If is clear that they aren't going to be famous friends or even polite to each other, just accept defeat and socialize with your friends when your guy is elsewhere.

THE BOY FRIEND

This is a tricky one, dear girl. While it can be helpful to have a male acquaintance to whom you can turn for advice and support, it can also be fraught with complications. Your man is guaranteed to feel insecure and jealous if you spend too much time with a boy friend. No matter how enlightened he is, he will not like it. Would you like it if he sought out another female to spend time with, no matter how platonic?

Of course you wouldn't.

That said, you *can* make and keep male friends. But tread lightly. Try to get together in groups or public places. Tell your guy in advance that you are meeting your friend, tell him if you accidentally ran into him at the corner store, tell him if you have a hilarious phone conversation. Get the picture? Tell him everything. That harmless cup of coffee could have been seen by him or someone else; if it slips your mind when telling him about your day, suspicion will creep into his thoughts.

Of course, if the two of them are friends, things are bound to be smoother. Hang out together. Double date. Send them off together for some quality time on the golf course. But don't take it for granted that your man is completely secure. Make sure your guy knows he comes first and that you think he is the most insightful, humorous, kind, handsome man you have ever met. Offhand comments like "Peter is the most motivated person—he just started his own business while training for a marathon" will strike a direct blow to your guy's ego.

Of course, if your male friend happens to prefer, well, men, forget everything you just read. Treat him as you would your most fashionable and sage gal pal and make sure your love knows which team your chum plays for.

BEING THE HOSTESS

Like a girl scout, it pays to be prepared. You never know when your man, no matter how well you've trained him, will bring home a friend, co-worker, or boss. And your friends might need to drop in unannounced if there's a crisis brewing. Always cook enough for a surprise guest (after all, men love leftovers anyway). Make sure you always have a tray of steaks or a bag of frozen shrimp in the freezer; you can always defrost them in the microwave at a pinch—it's better than having nothing to serve.

When a guest shows up on your doorstep, greet them with a welcoming smile, take their coat, and offer them a beverage. If they caught you in the middle of a troublesome task, do not let your stress or irritation show. Dust yourself off, swipe on a bit of lipstick and act as if there's nothing you'd like better than a visit from your guest. They may need to talk, they may just want a "fix" of your warmth and charm, or they may have simply been passing by. In any event, you will certainly have a better time if you lay aside your surprise at their intrusion and view it as an unexpected gift.

To that end, it pays to be somewhat prepared. It's not a bad idea to live as though you are always entertaining (even if you're only entertaining yourself and your man). Have regular meals at the table so you don't forget how to set a table, let alone eat properly at one. Have candles, soothing background music, and cut flowers on hand; it adds incomparable ambiance should a guest appear—and they can also enliven your mealtimes, especially when you have not had dinner together for a while, or when it's a weekend. It's easy to forget about table manners and cloth napkins when you're eating in front of the television every night.

BE PREPARED

If you welcome and can lay out a spread for surprise guests and impromptu gatherings, you'll be the most popular hostess on the block. Here are pantry items to have on hand for games, movie nights, and unexpected visitors:

CHECKLIST

- ☑ Cold beer
- ☑ Single-malt scotch
- ☑ Club soda, ginger ale, seltzer and other mixers
- ☑ Preferred drink ingredients for close friends
- ☑ Plenty of ice
- ☑ Salsa
- ☑ Tortilla chips
- ☑ Pretzels
- ☑ Party dip packets
- ☑ Crackers
- ☑ Cheeses
- ☑ Deli meats (salami keeps well)
- ☑ Mixed nuts
- ☑ Frozen party nibbles like sausage rolls, mini quiches, chicken strips, and the like
- ☑ Frozen tray of lasagna (see recipe on page 34)
- ☑ Ice cream
- ☑ Cookie dough (to make cookies in a jiff, not to eat)
- ☑ Coffee

In addition to basic foodstuffs and drinks, outfit your home with the following:

CHECKLIST

- ☑ Two televisions (you never know when your guy wants to watch a game when you're having a movie night!)
- ☑ Stereo system
- ☑ Glassware: plenty of wine, pilsner, and martini glasses that match (inexpensive ones that can be replaced if broken)
- ☑ Party ware: platters, trays, cocktail napkins, chip-and-dip bowls, cheese slicer, toothpicks
- ☑ Varied CD collection to match any mood
- ☑ Candles and candle holders
- ☑ Firewood and kindling (if you have a fireplace)
- ☑ Good table linen
- ☑ At least two decks of cards
- ☑ Various board games
- ☑ Tissues and extra rolls of toilet paper
- ☑ Extra-large cushions or spare fold-out chairs
- ☑ Cocktail shaker
- ☑ Spare string of fairylights to pull out for a special event
- ☑ Plenty of side tables/coffee tables for guests to place their drinks
- ☑ Vases for fresh flowers
- ☑ Caterers' packs of aluminum foil and plastic wrap for keeping food fresh

WHEN FRIENDS GET FRESH

Be firm but fair with his bachelor friends. If you frequently socialize, it's likely that one or more of his rambunctious pals will drink too much and lose all sense of reason. In other words, he may get fresh with you in word or in deed.

This is not good. *Ever.*

Set ground rules up front. Although it should be obvious, some young men need to be reminded that you are spoken for and that while you do appreciate compliments and camaraderie, you do not tolerate propositions or bottom pats, no matter how drunk, depressed, or high-spirited they may be.

Whenever a friend tries to get chummy with you in a way you find inappropriate, remove his arm or lips, step away, and tell him he is making you uncomfortable. Explain that you enjoy his friendship and do not want to limit your contact with him in the future. He either needs to back off or you will be forced to withdraw your company.

If he has been drinking, he probably will not register what you are saying so restate your feelings when he has sobered up. He will most likely be embarrassed and will respect your restraint and honesty. Resist the temptation to chalk the incident up to inebriation and let it slide.

Be open with your guy when his friend goes too far. This isn't the sort of information that he will want to find out about at a later date. Tell him that you took care of the situation but you wanted him to know about it. Explain that the pass was unrequited. Let him deal with it in whatever way he sees fit.

THE PARTY PRINCIPLES

For a lady of taste and grace, throwing parties is one of life's true pleasures.

But before the party, there is the preparation.

This is not so pleasant.

A hostess should be available during her party to mingle, introduce guests, and have a splendid time. Otherwise, why entertain at all? To be fully present at a function, you must plan.

First of all, decide what kind of party you want to have and then go from there.

Party	Food and drink	Decoration	Music
Dinner	Your signature dish, good wine	Cloth tablecloths and good china	Jazz
Cocktail	Hot appetizers, one signature cocktail	Cool swizzle sticks, retro throw pillows	Rat pack
Big bash	Chips & dip, beer	None. Put the breakables away	Dance, hip hop
Brunch	Frittata, fresh fruit	White tablecloth, fresh flowers	Classical, jazz
Superbowl or other sports final	Snack food, chicken wings, beer	Your team's memorabilia	The TV!
Barbecue	Kebabs, gin & tonics	Checkered tablecloth, citronella candles	Classic rock
House-warming	Finger food, wine and beer	Choose a theme	Jazz to begin, then dance as the night progresses

BE A GUEST AT YOUR OWN PARTY

The hostesses who become legend are those ladies who never—to put it indelicately—let their guests see them sweat. As anyone who's hosted an event knows, throwing a party is a *job*. The details are endless, the expense is considerable, and your time seems to be gobbled up by phone calls, multiple trips to the shopping center, and rearranging the furniture. But once the first guest arrives, the best hostess relaxes and remembers why she wanted to have the party in the first place: because they're *fun*! To continue the metaphor, don't sweat the small stuff. Things may get broken, a guest might be without a drink for a few minutes, and the music may cease. The important thing is to seek out quality conversation with each guest, be it for five or 30 minutes. If you keep your eye on the fun prize, you'll be the consummate hostess, your party will be a smashing success, and your guests will be falling over themselves to secure an invitation to a future gathering.

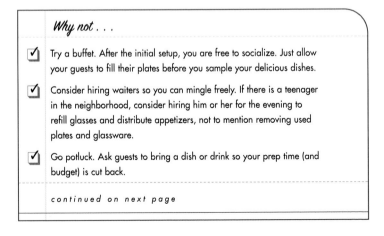

Why not . . .

- ☑ Try a buffet. After the initial setup, you are free to socialize. Just allow your guests to fill their plates before you sample your delicious dishes.

- ☑ Consider hiring waiters so you can mingle freely. If there is a teenager in the neighborhood, consider hiring him or her for the evening to refill glasses and distribute appetizers, not to mention removing used plates and glassware.

- ☑ Go potluck. Ask guests to bring a dish or drink so your prep time (and budget) is cut back.

continued on next page

continued

✓ Give guests roles, be it the game master, grill king, doorman, or barmaid. They'll be delighted to help out.

✓ Cheat on the food. Buy takeout, hide the containers (consider driving the evidence to a nearby dumpster), and dress up the food to avoid detection. From fried chicken and cornbread to guacamole and pasta salad, restaurants, delicatessens, and grocery stores stock down-home and exotic foodstuffs for your gathering. Doctor up your dishes with spices and garnish with fresh herbs.

PARTY CHECKLIST

✓ What kind of event are you hosting?

✓ How many people to invite?

✓ Guest list created and confirmed with your man?

✓ Set a date, time, and location

✓ Invitations: paper, e-mail, phone? RSVP necessary?

✓ Overall budget

✓ Food list

✓ Decoration, supplies list

✓ Beverage list (don't forget mixers)

✓ One week before the party: Make sure everyone's been invited, stock up on non-perishables, decorations, supplies, select outfit

✓ Day before the party: Confirm RSVPs, go grocery shopping, clean the house, etc.

✓ The day of the party: Buy fresh ingredients, flowers, decorate, prepare food dishes, shower, look radiant

As we've said, it's important for a hostess to focus on having a good time at her own party. Preparation can ensure that the party is on auto-pilot. However, there are a few guidelines that a hostess can benefit from, no matter what kind of gathering she's throwing. Obviously, your guy should share in the hosting duties and allocating areas of responsibility can help you divide and socially conquer. Give guests instructions as you take their coats so they can find their own way to snacks, amusements, and other guests.

Top Ten Rules to Hostess Success

1	Glasses must always be full.
2	Lighting must be low and flattering in all rooms, including the bathroom.
3	Food to be varied and plentiful, and spread throughout the party space.
4	Music to play continuously, at a volume suitable for conversation (unless dancing is afoot).
5	Hostess to dress the part.
6	Hostess to make the host shine.
7	The host and hostess should divide and conquer. Split up and reconnect at the end of the evening to recap over a nightcap.
8	Introduce guests to each other by relating an interesting fact about each one that gives a topic for a conversational point of entry.
9	Mingle. Avoid lingering too long in one place or with one person.
10	Don't sweat the small stuff. If someone breaks or damages something, smile and reassure your guest. Belongings can be repaired easier than relationships or hurt feelings.

THE IN-LAWS ISSUE

Ahhh, family. What used to be a safe haven has now, occasionally, become a den of doubt, if not outright opposition. And not just from his side. Your family believes you to be a precious pearl, because you are. It will be hard to convince your parents that your man is your equal. You must give them time to discover the wonderful qualities about him that you love . . . and vice versa. And they will.

So instead, turn your attention toward wooing your in-laws. Don't hit them over the head with attention and fuss. Instead, fall back on your impeccable manners. Take their lead on physical and verbal intimacy, that is, hug them if they hug you, call them by their first name if they invite you to do so. Respecting their boundaries and comfort level will go a long way to endearing you to them. Compliment their home, play with their pet, clean your plate, no matter how questionable a cook your mother-in-law is.

And invite them into your home. Make them feel welcome. Ask them for their advice on homemaking or interior decoration or communicating with your guy. This will subtly drive home the point that you are not trying to take their son away or competing with them for his affection. Rather, you are creating a home for your man and where they too can be comfortable spending time.

But not so comfortable that they want to live with you! Adding a layer of complication such as inviting family to move in may wreak havoc on hearth and home. Seek instead a solution should they need to change their living arrangements. Perhaps they can move closer to you or in an assisted living location. Maybe you can arrange for frequent visits to lend a hand and keep them company. But do not be swayed by guilt or passive disapproval; there are always more than one option if everyone is open-minded.

MOTHER DEAR OR MOTHER FEAR?

Your mother may well be your closest confidante. You may tell her everything. She wants you to be happy and is thrilled that you've settled down with a good guy. But she has only *your* best interests at heart. So like your friends, take care when over-sharing with your mom. At the slightest sign that he isn't treating you like you deserve—even if it's an isolated incident—your mother will find ways to discourage the relationship (if she secretly thinks you can do better) or to defend his actions (if she is worried about you being single again). Be discreet in confiding things about your guy and your relationship. Even better, ask questions about how your mom has dealt with the issues surrounding living with a man. As she shares her experiences, she'll feel appreciated, and you can remain vague in your concerns.

It may take a while for your man and your mom to warm to each other. Don't take sides. This is a no-win situation, as you love them both and will either defend their actions or try to convince each of the other's qualities. They must discover what kind of relationship is comfortable for both of them. All you can do is give them time opportunities.

As far as his mother, she will think her boy can do no wrong. Seek out time with your mother-in-law, either in a group setting or alone. Ask her to share baby photos or childhood stories about him. This will demonstrate that while you love him, you don't know everything about him. You certainly haven't known him as long or as well as she has, so respect that. Show an interest in her outside of her being your beloved's mother. You may find that you like her and would seek out her friendship, regardless of your relationship with her son. But you have a common link to start from: you love the same man. Build upon that foundation and the relationship will grow from there.

CHAPTER

6

STARTING A FAMILY

In this chapter, you'll learn how to:

✻ Decide when it's time to have a baby ✻ Ease your man into the idea of fatherhood ✻ Keep romance thriving after parenthood ✻ Cope with the different behavior your man will show a son versus a daughter

IT'S A LAW OF NATURE, ONE THAT KEEPS OUR SPECIES GOING. When you love someone and are committed to them, thoughts naturally turn to creating a family. Perhaps you have already discussed it at length and know it's something you both want. Perhaps not. If you foresee having children with your man, but you don't know how he feels, it can be nerve-wracking to bring up the topic. Be honest, gentle, and ease him into the subject. Discuss all the ways you'll keep the spark of romance in your lives, even with the added responsibility of children. Stroke his ego about what he can offer as a parent. And revel in the sense of excitement and deepening commitment that comes with contemplating your future family.

FOOLS RUSH IN

Certainly "surprises" happen, but it is much more desirable to plan your pregnancy and get used to the idea slowly. Not sure how your man feels about having kids? A good way to start assessing his readiness is to see how he reacts to small children that you encounter in your lives. When you're enjoying a lovely outing together, point out adorable children you see along the way. Watch his reaction when he's around children or holding babies at family gatherings, and gauge his level of enthusiasm when a sibling or close friend announces a pregnancy. If you have friends or relatives with great kids, plan a visit. A fun day spent with a happy family is a great segue into, "What do you think about us having children?" Indicate that you're ready for a dialog on the subject, without harping on it. Allow him to come around.

Once you've established that a family is something you both want, don't go crazy right away. Turning the spare room into a nursery overnight or buying a boatload of pregnancy books or baby toys might give any man a serious anxiety attack. Instead, entice him. Let him know what a good father you think he will be. Tell him the characteristics you hope your child inherits from him. Offer stories of other couples who travel, go to dinner, and enjoy each other even though they have kids. And of course, explain to him how much fun it will be trying to conceive—and that a lot of sex will be involved. *A lot.*

Next, think about a timeline. Unless you have medical reasons to hurry things along, take your time discussing when would be the best time to conceive. Have fun with it. Imagine your lives a year from now, then three years, or five years from now. Do you imagine a house full of kids by then? Or maybe just one newborn? Talk about your expectations and hopes. It's okay to daydream and it's okay to talk about the little things. Does he love the idea of twins? What would you name your children? Who do you think they will look like? Fantasizing, especially when you're in the comfort zone of your own bed or snuggled up on the couch, can be the first step in getting ready for a baby. Let yourselves luxuriate in the *idea* of a child before committing to the real thing.

Then there's the nitty-gritty. Can your home, financial situation, and career track handle a child? Do you feel you've had enough time as a couple on your own? Have you discussed your viewpoints and opinions on childrearing? Do you have family or friends nearby on whom you can rely for help? While there's rarely an "ideal time" to have a child the two of you should be on the same page about the logistics, emotional readiness, and basic timeline before conceiving. While you may be nervous about the responsibility of parenthood, you should both also feel truly excited by it. Once you have a child, it's forever. Make sure that you—and your relationship—are ready for it.

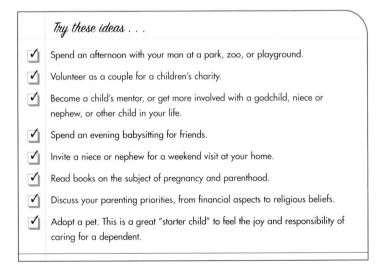

Try these ideas . . .

- ☑ Spend an afternoon with your man at a park, zoo, or playground.
- ☑ Volunteer as a couple for a children's charity.
- ☑ Become a child's mentor, or get more involved with a godchild, niece or nephew, or other child in your life.
- ☑ Spend an evening babysitting for friends.
- ☑ Invite a niece or nephew for a weekend visit at your home.
- ☑ Read books on the subject of pregnancy and parenthood.
- ☑ Discuss your parenting priorities, from financial aspects to religious beliefs.
- ☑ Adopt a pet. This is a great "starter child" to feel the joy and responsibility of caring for a dependent.

BABY YOUR MAN

Your man is a child at heart. He may not admit it, but he enjoys being mothered by you. Like a boy, he loves it when you make him a sandwich, run him a bath, surprise him with a treat, and care for him when he's sick. In most relationships, the woman is the primary nurturer, caring for both the home and the relationship in an instinctively maternal way. Because of this, it's no surprise that when a man resists the idea of children, there's often an unspoken reason: he worries about losing your nurturing attention; he's afraid of having to share your love and your energy; and he's resistant to the idea of not being the center of your world.

Who can blame him?

Remember that you have the ability to ease his fears, even when he doesn't verbalize them. Assure him, at every turn, that you have enough love to go around. Discuss other mothers you plan to emulate, and how they make time for their relationship as well as their kids. Let him know that you can establish ground rules and traditions as a couple to make sure you keep the romance alive, even after you have children— from committing to a monthly date night to ensuring a bedtime schedule that allows for intimacy.

Admittedly, your schedule will become erratic and busy with the introduction of children into your lives. That's why it's imperative to carve time out to spend with each together. Treat it as you would an appointment with a client. And if at all possible, get out of the house. Hire a babysitter (or if you have trust issues, ask a relative or friend to watch the kids), go out to dinner, and stare into each other's eyes. Go to a movie and snuggle up to him in the dark. Take a walk on the beach and enjoy a scream-free zone as you listen to the waves. Schedule in time to be spontaneous, as contrary as that may sound.

DON'T LET KIDS RULE THE ROOST

Even before you have children, you can reassure your man that your relationship won't take a backseat. Talk about what's most important to you as you get ready for parenthood. Use this list as a springboard to useful discussion on the subject.

After we have a baby, is it important that we . . .

✓	Still travel?	✓	If so, what kinds of places can we go that are both appealing to us and baby-friendly?
✓	Have regular dates?	✓	If so, how often?
✓	Set a firm bedtime for our children?	✓	If so, should we also establish a set time that we go to the bedroom?
✓	Keep the house in order?	✓	If so, is a maid or cleaning service an option?
✓	Maintain close relationships with our friends?	✓	If so, how can we ensure this?
✓	Maintain some independence?	✓	If so, should each parent have a monthly "free night" to get out of the house, see friends, or pursue hobbies?
✓	Are still dedicated to a demanding career?	✓	If so, what compromises can be made for the sake of everyone's sanity?

THE STORK HAS LANDED

You've probably read innumerable books, had a few baby showers, and turned the spare bedroom into a nursery fully stocked with blankets and toys. But how do to mentally prepare for such a profound change at home? You barely have enough time for your other baby (your man, dear).

Your baby will take over your life and most likely your home. Early on, make an effort to contain the chaos by creating a nursery, complete with toy chest and bureau, for your little one. If need be, get creative about maximizing your ever-shrinking space. Hide pacifiers and rattles behinds books and in cupboards, much like you store lipsticks, so you'll never be caught without a way to soothe the little savage. Think through your storage systems for clothes, diapers, toys, and other equipment before the baby arrives.

You will undoubtedly designate an area for your nursery. Prepare your baby's room as early as possible. Not only will your man be pulled into the excitement by selecting stuffed animals and painting a colorful mural on the wall, a nursery can serve as a closet of sorts until the baby makes his or her appearance. When friends and family shower you with baby gifts, they can pile up and take over your home if you aren't vigilant and if you don't have a space carved out and prepared early on.

If the cost of all this new gear gives you the jitters, consider other options. Basinettes and baby clothes can be useful one month, but obsolete the next once baby grows out of them. Ask friends with older children to lend you their secondhand gear. Or check out secondhand shops or online auctions for this kind of equipment.

NURSERY THEMES

No matter if it's a boy or a girl, these creative motifs can make any nursery a magical place for your baby. If you don't have a lot of artistic talent, use stencils or paint quotes from your favorite childhood books on the walls to keep your baby—and you—inspired.

Theme	How to decorate
Jungle	Paint friendly lions, tigers, elephants, and monkeys peeking through tall grasses and bushes.
Nautical	Paint your walls a deep blue and dot a wall with waves, sailboats, and a lighthouse.
Forest	Place a couple of faux trees (or potted trees) in the corners that you can sit under with your baby when reading books.
Garden	Paint bright big blooms on the walls for a stimulating environment.
Outer space	Aliens are always nifty.
Family tree	Start a genealogy tree on the wall.
Beach	If you're not averse to cleaning, how about an indoor sandbox or a beach umbrella?
Geography	Cover a wall with a huge map of your country, state, or town.
Zoo	Large stuffed animals create a wild menagerie.
Circus	Paint elephants, clowns, acrobats, lion tamers, and a ringmaster on the walls; paint a big top on the ceiling.
Under the sea	Paint sea creatures, both real and imaginary, on the wall; add a fish mobile and an aquarium.

LIVING WITH A MAN LIVING WITH A BABY

Consider doing the tasks of feeding, changing, and bathing baby together with your man a few times until you both have the hang of it and feel comfortable going solo. Here are some pointers for getting into the mindset of your man and easing him gently out of it.

Task	How he views it	How to explain it to him
Warming a bottle	Tedious	You know how you feel if your favorite beer is too warm? Well, that's how he feels when his bottle isn't the right temperature!
Changing a diaper	More disgusting than that scene in *Alien*	How would you feel if you had a toilet strapped to your bum?
Bathtime	Boring	This is the baby's version of a pool or jacuzzi, and at least poop isn't involved (usually).
Burping	Unnecessary	You view belching as one of life's greatest pleasures, so think about how she must feel after eating a jar of pureed carrots.
Feeding	Messy	It's the food fight you never had in the college cafeteria.
Putting the baby down	Takes too long (the game's going to start in 10 minutes)	Use that time to say the silly things to her you don't want anyone to hear.

BONDING WITH BABY

Once you made eyes with your new addition, you were hooked. And you know your man is over the moon about your child. However, he might be treading lightly around the baby, unsure of his role in the household and, frankly, afraid of dropping the baby on his or her head. It's going to be up to you to include him in child care from the start. While you are expecting, it's reasonable to expect that your guy learn as much about babies, pregnancy, and parenting as possible. Instead of the latest thriller, take turns reading aloud a chapter from a childcare book before bedtime.

When the baby comes, carve out small blocks of time for your man and little one to bond on their own. Trust that he'll ask for help if he needs it. Be warned, though, that if you don't involve him and hand over responsibility now and again, he will regard you as the primary caregiver and be reluctant to assist, especially when it's 3 a.m. or when his buddies drop by. Don't enable this behavior! Once you are confident that he knows how to perform key parenting functions, give yourself a break and leave the house for a few hours so he can bond properly with his pride and joy.

If you find, as many couples do, that your relationship is having a hard time in the midst of new-baby mania, or that you or your man is having a hard time bonding with baby, don't be afraid to ask for help—from your parents or his, from understanding friends, or a dedicated organization which provides advice and a helping hand for new parents. A few hours off baby-minding duty for the two of you to reconnect and discuss how things are going will make all the difference.

KEEPING ROMANCE ALIVE

Once you become a mother, it's natural that your focus will shift to your child. But it's absolutely vital that you do not forget your man, and your romantic life as a couple. While you'll certainly be tired and distracted in your new role, keep in mind that small things will mean a lot to your man. By taking just a little time out of your hectic mommy schedule, you'll show him that he's still the king of the castle—and of your heart.

Try these ideas . . .

☑ Don't let yourself go. Just slipping into an attractive top moments before he comes home will make an impression, as will lipstick and freshly brushed hair.

☑ Pamper yourself when you can. While he's caring for the baby, give yourself a quick manicure, a fragrant bubble bath, or a facial. If you can, slip away to the salon or spa for some fresh highlights or a lash/eyebrow tint. He'll notice your revived appearance and you'll feel refreshed.

☑ Order dinner in. Place the call before he gets home, and remember to order his favorite dishes. For a small price and little effort, he'll feel taken care of when he smells the kung-pao chicken and you hand him his favorite beer, rather than coming home to an empty kitchen.

☑ Be attentive in the boudoir. Don't forget the power of lingerie, soft music, candles, and a bedroom free of baby toys or stacks of laundry. Take ten minutes to set the stage, and you'll both reap the rewards.

☑ Take time to do the simple things you loved to do before the baby came along, like rubbing each other's feet on the couch, taking a stroll, or picking up scones and coffee for Sunday breakfast—all still doable with a baby.

continued on next page

continued

 Consider hired help. Whether it's a diaper service, a cleaning service, or a laundry service, the expense is worth the extra time to enjoy a conversation— or some snuggling—with your man.

 Hire a babysitter. It may be hard at first, but if you start a monthly ritual of a day or night to yourselves, it will only get easier. Don't be tempted to use the free time to do household tasks or overdue errands. Instead, go to the restaurant where you had your first date, or dress up and have drinks at a new bar.

DADDY'S GIRL OR CHIP OFF THE OLD BLOCK

What difference does your baby's gender make, when it comes to your man's parenting techniques?

If she's Daddy's Girl, watch for . . .

- ✓ Your man's inability to discipline his daughter and hold firm on household rules
- ✓ Your man's frequent "giving in" to her whims, including buying presents or candy she doesn't need
- ✓ Your man falling victim to feminine attributes (pouting, crying, batting her eyelashes) when she wants to get her way
- ✓ Your man relying on you to be "bad cop"
- ✓ Your man being distant or shy around his child, because girls are something of a mystery to him
- ✓ Your man encouraging female stereotypes, by praising beauty over brains or athletics in his daughter
- ✓ Your man being overprotective

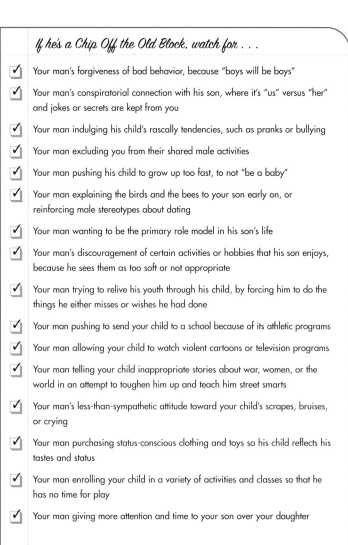

If he's a Chip Off the Old Block, watch for . . .

☑ Your man's forgiveness of bad behavior, because "boys will be boys"

☑ Your man's conspiratorial connection with his son, where it's "us" versus "her" and jokes or secrets are kept from you

☑ Your man indulging his child's rascally tendencies, such as pranks or bullying

☑ Your man excluding you from their shared male activities

☑ Your man pushing his child to grow up too fast, to not "be a baby"

☑ Your man explaining the birds and the bees to your son early on, or reinforcing male stereotypes about dating

☑ Your man wanting to be the primary role model in his son's life

☑ Your man's discouragement of certain activities or hobbies that his son enjoys, because he sees them as too soft or not appropriate

☑ Your man trying to relive his youth through his child, by forcing him to do the things he either misses or wishes he had done

☑ Your man pushing to send your child to a school because of its athletic programs

☑ Your man allowing your child to watch violent cartoons or television programs

☑ Your man telling your child inappropriate stories about war, women, or the world in an attempt to toughen him up and teach him street smarts

☑ Your man's less-than-sympathetic attitude toward your child's scrapes, bruises, or crying

☑ Your man purchasing status-conscious clothing and toys so his child reflects his tastes and status

☑ Your man enrolling your child in a variety of activities and classes so that he has no time for play

☑ Your man giving more attention and time to your son over your daughter

CHAPTER

7

THE OTHER WOMAN

In this chapter, you'll learn how to:

* Control your jealousy * Distinguish between a real threat and a platonic pal * Mark your territory * Keep his attention, whether you are there in person or in spirit

JEALOUSY IS DEFINITELY NOT AN ATTRACTIVE QUALITY.
Rather than conveying how much you love your man, the green-eyed monster only reveals your insecurity.

Rely on your instinct. If you sense your man is pulling away slightly, you are probably correct. You can usually tell if he's busy or stressed. However, you may be off the mark about the reason. It may very well be that he is troubled about his job or health, or a secret a friend made him promise not to share with anyone, including you. He may be experiencing cold feet because he wants to take your relationship to the next level and that scares him, no matter how madly he adores you. Let common sense prevail.

USE YOUR HEAD . . .

Pick a time when your man seems relaxed and open to conversation—not right after work, and certainly not when you've been bickering about something else. Let him know how important he is to you, and that you hope that you can always be a shoulder for him to lean on. Remind him that you love him unconditionally, and that he can share anything with you—even worries about your relationship. Many men simply have a hard time starting a conversation when emotions are involved. If you gently invite him to open up, and remind him that he has a safe place to do so (i.e., you won't overreact to what he has to say), he may begin to reveal his deeper thoughts to you.

If you feel jealousy or uncertainty welling up inside you, take a few deep breaths and ask yourself a few questions.

CHECKLIST

- [x] Has your man been acting strangely?
- [x] Has he become incommunicative or less physical?
- [x] Is he vague when telling you about his day?
- [x] Is there a woman you suspect has designs on him?

If you answered "no" to these questions, just keep an eye on the situation, keep the lines of communication open, and continue to be your loving self.

If you answered "yes" to even one of these questions, take a few deep breaths, get a massage, and quietly go about shoring up your defenses.

. . . BUT TRUST YOUR GUT

If talking to him gets you nowhere, you can do a little detective work if you suspect your man may be engaging in hanky-panky. Be careful, however, not to let your mistrust completely destroy the trust that the two of you share.

Sleuthing Tips

CHECKLIST

- ✓ Look for his credit card statements and phone bills. Are they hidden? If not, check for any unusual expenses or numbers on them.

- ✓ Log his behavior and appearance for a week. Does he head straight for the shower when he comes home? Does he ever smell different, perhaps with a hint of a strange perfume on him? Does he work late more frequently than usual? Does he avoid eye contact with you at times?

- ✓ Seduce him. Is he receptive or shut down to your advances?

- ✓ Try to call him late in the day. If he's at work, he should pick up. If he's unreachable, leave a message and take note of his response time.

- ✓ If you feel comfortable doing this (i.e., are feeling a bit desperate), look through his wallet, pockets, briefcase, appointment book, or cell phone log for phone numbers, credit card receipts, business cards, and the like. Analyze his shirt collars for signs of makeup, sniff his clothing for perfume or other scents that may bear evidence of physical contact.

- ✓ Analyze his friends and coworkers. If they avoid eye contact or make excuses to flee the scene, they may know that your man is being unfaithful in mind or body.

TANTRUMS

Throwing a tantrum will get you nowhere. Well-placed tears, however, can be an effective weapon in a woman's armory. Looking out of control or wildly jealous, let alone throwing breakables at his head—which is what you will most definitely feel like doing—will only result in him beating a hasty retreat from the home or fighting back. His first instinct is self-preservation and it will take time before he lowers his defenses and actually thinks about why you were upset in the first place.

Crying will drive home your vulnerability, so if you want to regain the power in the relationship, make sure that you have a sympathetic audience before releasing the dam. Sometimes you have to do the hard thing and battle to hold the floodgates back in order to get across a few well-selected words. If he is angry or non-responsive with you, crying may only result in distain on his part. However, if you have good reason to have hurt feelings because of something he did or didn't do, quietly shed a few tears in front of him and remind him of the many ways your life together is rewarding and *right*. Be specific in chronicling your best times. For example, remind him of how you laid in bed on that vacation to the shore, laughing yourself to tears over a sick joke. He will feel like a fool and want to do everything in his powers to make you stop crying as soon as possible. He may reassure you with words, through his actions, or by thoughtful gifts. And that's nothing to cry about!

If he doesn't attempt to dry your tears and is unmoved by your entreaties, he may well have thoughts of another woman. At this point, it is time to retrench and review your battle plan. A formidable rival may be threatening to destroy the home you have worked so very hard to create.

MARK YOUR TERRITORY

This may be an indelicate metaphor but we are way past propriety when it comes to protecting your relationship.

Don't leave it up to your guy to make it clear that he's taken. He may enjoy the flirtation and need to feel attractive to other women. You do not need to artfully drape yourself over him at the movies or stick your tongue in his ear at cocktail parties. There are more subtle ways to tell the world he's all yours.

CHECKLIST

- ☑ Kill all women with kindness. It's a bit harder to go after your man when you are their friend or extremely likable.

- ☑ Blot your lipstick on his collar. He may not see it but the world will.

- ☑ Buy a handsome, luxury watch for him. Whether he's checking the time or receiving yet another compliment on his timepiece, he will be thinking about you 24 hours a day.

- ☑ Endear his friends to you so they will be in your camp if trouble is brewing. They can act as spies, tell the woman to back off, or remind your man of the many ways you have changed his life for the better.

- ☑ Take impromptu photos that he'll get a kick out of putting in his office or wallet. Classic black-and-white photo booth strips will be more palatable to his manly demeanor than, say, a formal portrait of the two of you in a floral frame. The smaller the photo, the easier to fit in his wallet.

- ☑ Give him plenty of affection at home and invite him to share fantasies with you, so he doesn't have to pursue them elsewhere.

- ☑ Give him plenty of positive reinforcement and compliments.

- ☑ Keep things spicy by surprising him with new lingerie or a night in a hotel.

SWEET NOTHINGS

Color his world with reminders of you, strategically placed. Be subtle, however. Obvious attempts to keep your guy's eye will only give you an air of desperation. Small reminders of your life together, on the other hand, will reinforce what a good thing he has going with you. Who would want to mess with that?

Location	What to leave
Pillow	Photo of his favorite body part of yours
Steering wheel, visor, driver's seat	Gift certificate to his favorite coffee shop
His coat pocket	Tissue spritzed with your perfume
His briefcase or messenger bag	Note with a lipstick imprint
Voicemail	Invitation for a date night. Pique his interest with as few details as possible: "Tonight, 8:30, living room"
Cell phone	New start-up message every so often as a surprise
E-mail	Links to articles he'd be interested in
Computer	Valentine on his keyboard (do not mess with his desktop!)
Suitcase	Coupon for massage, redeemable upon his return
Gym bag	Workout CD of his favorite cheesy songs
Book	Bookmark the book he's currently reading with a top-ten list—of your favorite moments with him, of the adjectives you've used to describe him, whatever.
Toilet seat	Give new meaning to "bathroom humor." Write a fun message in a temporary marker or lipstick under the toilet seat for an unexpected treat.

KEEP HIM ON HIS TOES . . .

A subtle way to guarantee that he never takes you for granted is to ban predictability from your life. First of all, develop an unpredictable schedule. As crazy as it sounds, schedule in chunks of time to be spontaneous. Don't apprise him of your schedule unless he asks and then only keep to the specific query at hand. You will retain an air of mystery, even though you both share a bathroom.

As part of your unpredictability plan, occasionally pay him unexpected visits to deliver food or drop off a note. Each visit, however, should have a purpose. Don't just drop by his office to say hello. He may get the feeling you are checking up on him, rather than running a thoughtful errand or delivering a loving message.

Take a real interest in his work. Learn as much as you can about his industry, his company, and his specific position. It's surprising how many people don't have a clear idea of what their partner does all day. Read up on his field through the Internet, books, or professional journals he leaves lying about. Ask him questions. Ask him about his specialist areas of law, finance, construction—whatever—and get to know the names of his key coworkers. Most likely he will love sharing this important area of his life with you. If you get in the habit of recapping his day, he won't feel the slightest need to turn to someone else who "understands" what he goes through from nine to five.

BE the other woman. Trying on different personas—and wigs— can be as exhilarating to you as it is to him. Saunter up to him at the bar when he's having an after-work drink or at the market when he's buying groceries. Pretend to be a stranger and offer to buy him a drink or a box of cereal. He won't have eyes for anyone but the fetching redhead in aisle 3.

. . . BUT DON'T SMOTHER HIM

Your guy is with you because he wants to be. Trust that. Asking for reassurance, calling him frequently at work, wanting to spend every waking moment with him is a casebook technique to drive him away, perhaps into the arms of another woman.

Give him a bit of space so he thinks he has a modicum of free will. Saccharine as it may seem, there is some truth to the adage that if you love someone, set him free. If he comes back to you, he's yours. If he doesn't, he never belonged to you.

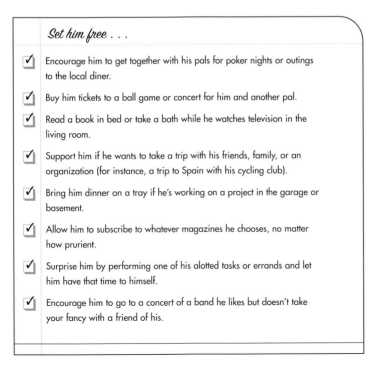

Set him free . . .

- ✓ Encourage him to get together with his pals for poker nights or outings to the local diner.

- ✓ Buy him tickets to a ball game or concert for him and another pal.

- ✓ Read a book in bed or take a bath while he watches television in the living room.

- ✓ Support him if he wants to take a trip with his friends, family, or an organization (for instance, a trip to Spain with his cycling club).

- ✓ Bring him dinner on a tray if he's working on a project in the garage or basement.

- ✓ Allow him to subscribe to whatever magazines he chooses, no matter how prurient.

- ✓ Surprise him by performing one of his aloted tasks or errands and let him have that time to himself.

- ✓ Encourage him to go to a concert of a band he likes but doesn't take your fancy with a friend of his.

UPGRADING YOUR MAN

In this chapter, you'll learn how to:

✱ Dress him more to your liking   ✱ Open up his world culturally
✱ Become his career coach and professional "running mate"
✱ Refine his manners

YOU KNOW YOUR MAN IS A GEM, BUT TO THE REST OF THE world he may look like a diamond in the rough. So what's a stylish girl to do? Shouldn't loving your man mean accepting him just as he is? Good heavens, no!

When setting out to transform your man, you must be subtle, you must be kind, and you must play to his strengths, tastes, and interests. If, for example, he loves punk rock and loathes golf, don't try to make him over as the king of prep. Think instead about how you can spiff up his edgy look.

You must resist an all-out effort to change your man. This is the path to abject misery. You were initially attracted to your guy "as is" and you should regard the guest bedroom as a massive fix-up project, not him. Think, rather, about the *specific* things you'd like to upgrade. It may be as small as his footwear or hair product, or as wide-ranging as poor manners. If you create a very targeted wish list, and if you keep in mind the timescale involved for real change to occur, you'll be able to polish your diamond in the rough without causing any permanent damage to his psyche or your relationship.

You will both have a better experience if you take it slow. Think about what he likes and what you like and how you can meet somewhere in between. Give him positive reinforcement: compliment him when you find him particularly handsome, when he chooses a gift you adore, thank him for accompanying you to the museum, or discuss the power dynamics that were flying at his company's cocktail party. If he knows you're interested in his cultural, physical, and career advancement, he'll be an enthusiastic partner in your plans. Pose your suggestions for change as questions. Ask him what he likes about his favorite clothes, music, or furnishings. You might even find that your tastes change slightly in the process . . . these things happen when you live with a man you love.

THE NO MAN'S LAND
OF SHOPPING

A savvy woman knows that before she shops with her man, she has to *know* her man. Before you step foot out of your home, do a little sleuthing. Check out what colors he tends to wear as well as what colors look great on him. Ask him what he likes when surfing online, watching TV, or flipping through magazines and catalogs.

Initially, silently accompany him when he's shopping for clothes. Is he impatient, forgoing the dressing room? Does he contemplate his image at length in the mirror? What details matter to him most (fit, color, trendiness, softness)? How much does he like to spend?

Think about which outfits of his you love. Do you prefer his weekend wear to his business attire? Is there one pair of trousers that you think fit him perfectly? Is there one physical feature of his you think should be highlighted or perhaps downplayed?

Take all of this information and merge it. Does your taste seem to match up with his sensibilities, or do you want him to wear clothes that are the antithesis of his current style? As a style maven, it is up to you to find common ground. You cannot urge him to don a conservative suit when he's used to his beloved polo shirts and khakis. Instead, focus on baby steps. If you suggest that he add a suit jacket to his current work look for meetings or chilly days, you may have a more receptive audience.

Once your sleuthing is complete, you can venture out for a shopping excursion. Take him to a department store. The choices are varied and he won't feel under attack from an overly solicitous sales associate looking for a sizable commission.

As suggested in chapter 4, pick out a few things you'd like him to try and ask him to do the same for you. If he's used to wearing pants with pleats, he may be reluctant to try on the flat-front trousers you're dying to get him into. Ask him to put them on just for kicks or to please him. Reassure him that no matter what he tries on, you won't push him to buy anything he doesn't like.

Men are creatures of habit. If he's been comfortable wearing the same brand of blue jeans or shirts for years, it's going to take some time. Be patient. Once you get him into a new look, he will see for himself how much trimmer, more successful, muscular, or swarthy he looks. If he puts on a color suited to his complexion or that brings out the color in his eyes, he should just glow. But if he can't see it, tell him! Have a sales assistant standing by to second your emotion, and try some of these specifics in your compliments:

"It brings out the color in your beautiful eyes."

"You look so manly."

"I never realized how muscular your thighs are."

"That shirt shows off your broad chest."

"Have you been working out?"

"You'll be beating women off with a stick!"

"You look like a million bucks."

"I didn't think it possible but you are even more handsome."

"What did you do with my man?"

"I'm speechless."

Pick out complete looks for him. If you pick out a shirt, trousers, belt, and loafers, he will get the whole effect when he tries something on and it will be harder for him to refuse to consider any one thing.

Once you have amassed a pile of garments for him to model, let him venture into the dressing room alone (unless he requests your assistance). Give him space.

When he's dressed, have him model each ensemble in front of you. Have him look at himself in a large mirror (a three-way one, if available). Point out the positives and negatives and be specific. Call attention to the hem of his trousers if it breaks perfectly over the top of his shoes. Tell him if the shirttail is too long and visually shortens his torso. Show him how the pleats of one pair of trousers are unflattering to his waistline when compared with the cut of another pair. Focusing on details will make him more aware of what complements his body as well as what hides his best features.

Be encouraged by any progress, no matter how small. It is natural to want your guy to look and feel the best he can, but this is an ongoing process. Remember that you have the rest of your lives to work this through and that the art of nurturing a well-dressed man is not something that you can expect to achieve overnight. Just think of the thousands of poor souls out there who don't have a style guru such as you to help them along. Part of the joy of living with a man is bringing out the best in them—and this means bringing out the best in the way they present themselves. Your man will come to appreciate the hints and gentle advice you offer him, but only if you are patient and willing to let him grow into his new look.

Do not become down in the mouth if he only buys a shirt on your first outing, and not the pants and sporty loafers you were also recommending. Take heart. The shirt may be in a style he's never before considered.

My goodness, you made significant headway just by getting him into the store and into clothing you picked out!

GETTING CULTURE

When he first courted you, you may have been wined and dined. You may have gone to movies, plays, concerts, and exhibitions.

Quite possibly, this has changed.

When you settle into domestic bliss, you may also become complacent in seeking out adventure. After all, living together is an adventure in and of itself! You have both been busy setting up house and meeting the daily challenges that are bound to crop up. And now you find yourself craving cultural experiences.

Getting your guy to take an interest in more cultural pursuits is not as difficult as it may seem at first blush. Pair the activity with his interests. For instance, if he is a sports buff, take him to a book signing for the latest best-selling sports biography.

Enroll in classes together. Many couples find classes or courses in wine tasting very fruitful. Develop your palate as you develop your knowledge of wine and each other. Or go to a free introductory ballroom dancing class. Most fellas won't object to a few hours of free instruction. If you get him to try something without obligation to continue, the pressure is off and he might actually have a good time instead of finding reasons to eschew the foxtrot.

Create traditions. If you have set up a regular date night or enjoy going out to dinner, take turns picking out restaurants to sample. He will be forced to peruse the newspapers or websites for new eateries. In doing so, he can't help but see other happenings around town. Buy a couple of sets of season tickets, one for his favorite sports team and one for your favorite theater or opera troupe. Reciprocity is key.

It probably won't be hard to get him to the movie theater, but ease him into plays. Start with comedies. As he becomes more enthusiastic or experimental, try the transition to dramas or musicals.

Art is more of a challenge. Gallery openings are a great way to get him into an artistic forum. There's usually food, drink, and lots of people so even if he isn't interested in the art at all, there is still something for him to do. And chances are that he'll contemplate some or all of the artwork during the event. Ask him a few questions just to see what he likes or how the art makes him feel. If you try to compare it to other artists or movements throughout history, he's going to feel out of place and skittish. But if you compare the subject of one painting to his favorite cartoon or the design of your tablecloth, he'll be able to have a comfortable point of reference. If there's an art exhibit at the museum you are desperate to see, "persuade" him to accompany you by taking him to lunch or dinner after you just "pop in" and check out the show. This works wonderfully if there's a major show in the big city. You can make a whole day of it and do something he likes in the city before or after you check out the exhibition.

If you want to go to	Try saying
A museum	"This painter expresses her sexuality through her art."
Dancing	"Dancing always makes me so amorous."
The ballet	"Dancers have the most amazing bodies."
The symphony	"Don't worry. The brass section will drown you out if you start snoring."
The opera	"There are Vikings, hot women, and lots of killing. Plus, you get to play with your binoculars."
A chick flick	"Women love a sensitive man who knows how to cry."
A book reading	"We can browse the magazine/music section afterwards."
Theater	"We can drink during intermission."

MAN ALIVE

Your guy is reasonably fit. He eats balanced meals. He plays ball with his buddies with some regularity. He drinks in moderation. You've even gotten him to wear sunscreen.

Okay, so he doesn't do *all* of these things. In fact, he wouldn't be caught dead with SPF on. But he has good intentions and his round edges make him a super snuggler. With a little behind-the-scenes effort on your part, you can ensure your guy is healthy, if not happy, for many years to come.

Let's start with his diet. He loves his snack foods. Keeping the refrigerator and his stomach filled with healthy alternatives will ease him out of his poor habits, at least until he goes to someone else's house. Pretzels are a great salty snack alternative to chips, since they have no fat. Fruit or raw vegetables don't seem to thrill the male appetite but a yummy fruit salad, coupled with a low-cal angel food cake, will make him forget he ever lived for cheesecake. Using low-fat versions of cream cheese, butter, oil, and the like won't even register with him. When cooking out, opt for ribs, chicken, fish filets, and anything that can be eaten without a bun. Again, subtly substituting ingredients or steering your guy away from high-fat, high-calorie, and high-carb foods will help keep him fit.

Don't be a nag when it comes to working out. Rather, incorporate exercise into your life together. Take regular walks after dinner, make gym dates, and take your bikes with you on vacations, no matter where you go. You might even suggest taking a martial arts class together. Taking the focus off the exercise is much easier when you're enthused about the activity.

With a little bit of ingenuity and a generous helping of care, you and your guy will be living and loving for quite some time.

DEVELOPING HIS AMBITION

You love your man dearly but do you find him lacking a certain fire in his belly? Does he seem complacent or uncaring about his job? Does he seem depressed at the thought of going to work on Monday?

While he may be thrilled with his relationship with you, career malaise can affect his attitude and confidence. And it's not a barrel of laughs for you, either. You might spend significant time listening to him detail his work woes or buoying up his spirits. And while you might want to offer professional advice, he might not want to hear it. You won't be able to take this for long. Resentment and frustration will eventually set in. If you are a positive person, you may resent his sour attitude. If you are a take-charge person, you may be frustrated by his unwillingness to take your advice or change his situation. Alternatively, he may enjoy his work and feel no need to seek out more responsibility or a better salary. If that's the case, try to bring the better job to him.

Take an interest in his work. Ask him questions over the dinner table. Research his industry. If he feels supported by you and that you have an excellent understanding of his profession, he will seek out your advice and value your opinions.

Support him by being the best partner-in-crime you can be. Join him at work functions. Think of yourself as his running mate. Casually network for him and keep your ear to the ground for opportunities.

Don't push him. The male species can be stubborn. He will dig his heels in and become further entrenched if you are too strident in your opinions. Be honest with him. Tell him that you are becoming frustrated by your inability to help him improve his situation. Convey to him that you want to be his helpmate but are unable to support him properly. Suggest he seek out career counseling. Ask him if you can help him research different positions or career paths.

GENTLEMANLY BEHAVIOR

Manners matter. While your man may be a pure gem, he may be of the "diamond in the rough" persuasion. He may not be a total brute but chances are he lacks an air of refinement. Of course he gets kudos for being a kind, financially solvent, funny, loving man. That's why he's worth investing in. He means well, dear boy. But he's never had a firm and loving hand leading him to the land of "Yes, ma'am" and "No, sir."

That's where you come in.

This is no small task. Teaching manners to a grown man is akin to teaching a horse to count. It goes against their nature but it's not impossible. Your man wants to please you, and if you kindly remind him when he offends your sensibilities or even embarrasses you, he'll soon learn to modify his behavior accordingly. He'll probably even start pointing out other boys who are displaying boorish behavior.

When he falls down on the gentleman job, there are several passive-aggressive things you can do to get him to fall in line, including waiting until he realizes his mistake and making snarky comments, such as "I simply *love* carrying all the groceries." The better solution is just to be honest and direct, no matter how hard it is. If he often goes ahead of you into stores and restaurants and fails to open the door, take matters into your own hands. Before the door swings back into your face yet again, ask him to open the door for you as you approach it. If you are walking down the street, ask him to walk next to the curb. Don't go into any lengthy explanations. If you continually ask him to display good manners in a considerate way, he will naturally incorporate more gentlemanly behavior. Be consistent in your requests. If you are erratic in your request, he will be confused as to how you want him to act. Or he will claim confusion . . . Either way, don't drop your guard even for a second.

THE GENTLEMAN'S CRIB SHEET

If necessary, photocopy this page and stick it in his jacket pocket or somewhere he will find it regularly so that he knows you want him to swot up on his manners.

Situation	What to do
Doors of any kind	Hold it open for a lady and allow her to go first
Lady enters the room	Stand
Lady joins the table	Stand and hold chair out for her
Lady leaves the table	Stand
Walking on sidewalk	Walk on outside, closest to curb
Chilly	Offer lady your coat
Lady is carrying bags and the like	Carry her packages
At a party or bar	Refill ladies' drinks
At the arcade	Win stuffed animal for lady (okay, this isn't required)
On a plane	Give lady choice of aisle or window seat
Bathroom	Leave the toilet seat down and wash hands after use
At dinner	Wait until everyone is served before eating
At end of evening	See lady safely home or hail her a cab and give her fare

SETTING YOUR MAN TO RIGHTS

Turn your caveman into a gentleman with a few well-placed and pointed comments. Drop these into conversation in a restrained tone of voice and he will realize the error of his ways immediately and seek to please you from that moment on.

Offence	What to say
Belches	"Is that your mating call?"
Chews gum with mouth open	"My mother always told me my face would freeze like that."
Spits	"There's been a drought. Thanks for helping the flowers grow."
Ignores coaster	"FYI: It will cost a week's wages to refinish that table."
Repositions his privates	"Baby, you don't need to draw my attention to that area. I'm always thinking about it."
Tips poorly	"Waiters remember poor tippers. Think about what they can do to your food the next time you come in. "
Starts eating before everyone's served	"I didn't realize you were so hungry."
Scratches his buttocks	"Would you like me to pick you up some diaper rash lotion?"
Forgets to say "please" and "thank you"	"Honey, what do you say to the nice lady/man?"
Doesn't hold the door open, chair out	Do not say anything. Just stand and wait.

ENJOY THE RIDE

Congratulations! You are now fully equipped to sail through the adventure of cohabitation with flying colors. But don't get too cocky.

Like anything that matters to you (your career, your figure, your garden), cultivating your relationship takes vigilance and effort. We often think that if it's the right relationship, everything will just take care of itself—as though you'd already done the hard work by nabbing your man. After reading this book, hopefully you'll realize at least one thing: even the best relationship takes constant—and of course enjoyable—work. Your relationship is no less a success because you stand guard over it and strive to improve it. Far from it. A subtle touch here and there will keep your household humming along and your friends wondering how you manage to have such a harmonious relationship. Keep them guessing.

During your journey into domestic bliss, take time to stop and savor your relationship. It can be tiring to be forever vigilant; in doing so, you can easily focus on the little things that irk you rather than the big things that make you swoon. When you spend time working on his poor grooming or tardiness, counter that by considering his unexpected kindnesses and his acceptance of your family. Looking at the bigger picture will give you the strength to go on tackling the unpleasantries.

Keep this book nearby so you can refer back to it in specific situations or when you have become lax in your relationship and need to develop a bit of strategy. It's not rocket science—you'll do fine in this crazy adventure. The important thing is to let love rule the roost. Like life, cohabitation is an ongoing journey and that journey matters more than the destination itself.

Enjoy living and loving together for years to come, but don't let your guard down for a minute!

INDEX